PARADISE LOST
BY ERIN SHIELDS

A theatrical adaptation of
Paradise Lost **by John Milton**

PLAYWRIGHTS CANADA PRESS
Toronto

For professional or amateur production rights, please contact:
Ian Arnold at Catalyst Talent Creative Management
312-100 Broadview Ave.
Toronto, ON M4M 3H3
416.645.0935, ian@catalysttcm.com

LIBRARY AND ARCHIVES CANADA CATALOGUING IN PUBLICATION
Shields, Erin, author
        Paradise lost / Erin Shields. -- First edition.

Play based on the poem Paradise Lost by John Milton.
Issued in print and electronic formats.
ISBN 978-1-77091-933-4 (softcover).--ISBN 978-1-77091-934-1 (PDF).--
ISBN 978-1-77091-935-8 (EPUB).--ISBN 978-1-77091-936-5 (Kindle)

        I. Milton, John, 1608-1674. Paradise lost. II. Title.

PS8637.H497P37 2018   C812'.6   C2018-903771-7
                                                  C2018-903772-5

Playwrights Canada Press acknowledges that we operate on land which, for thousands of years, has been the traditional territories of the Mississaugas of the New Credit, the Huron-Wendat, the Anishinaabe, Métis, and the Haudenosaunee peoples. Today, this meeting place is home to many Indigenous peoples from across Turtle Island and we are grateful to have the opportunity to work and play here.

We acknowledge the financial support of the Canada Council for the Arts— which last year invested $153 million to bring the arts to Canadians throughout the country—the Ontario Arts Council (OAC), the Ontario Media Development Corporation, and the Government of Canada for our publishing activities.

 Canada Council Conseil des arts
for the Arts   du Canada

 ONTARIO ARTS COUNCIL
CONSEIL DES ARTS DE L'ONTARIO
an Ontario government agency
un organisme du gouvernement de l'Ontario

 Canada

 Ontario
Ontario Media Development
Corporation

PARADISE LOST

ALSO BY ERIN SHIELDS

If We Were Birds
Mistatim / Instant
Soliciting Temptation

For Olive and Tallulah

FREEDOM AND THE FALL
by Paul Stevens

Paradise Lost is the single greatest poem in the English language. Its influence is pervasive. It can be felt in everything we know from old novels like *Frankenstein* or *Moby Dick* to present-day movies like *Blade Runner* or the Netflix thriller *The Fall*. When the poem was first published in 1667 people knew they were in the presence of something extraordinary. It's "the story of all things," wrote one admirer. It reveals "such a vast expanse of mind," said another. The poem was written by a blind man, the republican intellectual John Milton, and even his political enemies were ready to concede the poem's sublimity. Milton himself may be a "criminal and obsolete person," said the royalist MP Sir John Hobart, but "I never read anything more august, and withal more grateful to my (too much limited) understanding." Why would Hobart have felt so grateful?

In twelve books, each ranging from about six hundred to one thousand lines, Milton explains things we'd only half understood or perhaps glimpsed at through a glass darkly. He raises our consciousness. No work of art enables us to better understand the baffling complexity of evil. As a young man growing up just across the Thames from Shakespeare's Globe, his father being a trustee of the Blackfriars Theatre, Milton had originally wanted to write a great play, to rewrite the story of the Bible as a tragedy called *Adam Unparadized*. But in the event he became more ambitious and wrote it in the form of a classical epic, a poem to rival such revered works as Virgil's *Aeneid*. Despite its narrative form, the poem is still inherently dramatic, told from radically different, conflicting perspectives, both human and divine. Even the Devil seems to get his due. Satan, who is modelled on characters like Macbeth or Faustus, often thinks of himself as the hero, as a kind of Aeneas in his struggle to defeat God and establish a new community on earth.

What is immediately evident is that Milton is not the servant of his sources but their master. He makes one text speak to another in such a way that his ancient materials speak directly to the concerns of his seventeenth-century English audience, whether they be religious, political, or domestic. This insight, the liberation of the author to create as he or she needs, is central to Erin Shields's wonderful contemporary adaptation of Milton's early modern poem. She has learned from him and does what he did.

The subject of Milton's poem is the problem that haunts all the great religions or systems of thought: how to make sense of our experience of the strange world in which we live, how to transform our experience of fatality into continuity and contingency into meaning. In Christianity the problem takes the form of this question: If the loving God who created us is so good and all powerful, why are our lives filled with conflict, frustration and suffering; most importantly, why do we have to grow old and die?

In answering it, Milton focuses on the issue of human agency or free will. No one who knows anything, he says in one of his most impassioned pamphlets, "can be so stupid to deny that all men naturally were born free, being the image and resemblance of God himself, and were by privilege above all the creatures, born to command and not to obey." If this is the case, what went wrong? For Milton, what went wrong is our self-regarding failure to understand the limits of the agency we'd been granted. In overestimating our powers, in trusting absolutely in the freedom of our will or our ability to re-create the world in the image of desire, we actually frustrate that desire, destroy our freedom and produce every evil from climate change to nuclear war. The source of evil is, then, the degree to which we come to idolize our own freedom. In *Paradise Lost*, Milton aims to show how Adam and Eve, when they prefer their freedom to God's, quite literally bring death into the world.

In adapting Milton's poem, Erin Shields rewrites it as a play, if not quite the one Milton had in mind. She has no desire to speak to a seventeenth-century English audience. She wants to speak to us and she has no difficulty contesting some of Milton's "sacred truths." The tone changes, angels often sound like Bottom and the mechanicals from *A Midsummer Night's Dream*, and God, far from being omnipotent and omniscient, often seems overly defensive and worried about his own performance. Shields takes up hints from the poem and develops them to produce a kind of lighthearted irreverence. In Milton, paradise is an Arcadian version of England; it might be Jane Austen's country estate, Pemberley—"a happy rural seat of various view" with "lawns or level downs" and grazing sheep. In Shields, paradise is much edgier, distinctly Canadian with awe-inspiring mountains always threatened by pipelines and primeval forests by clear-cutting. There are lots of Ontario loons, wetlands and mud.

Most importantly, gender relations in Milton are hierarchized and clearly bounded—loving and companionate as Milton's Adam and Eve are, they are "not equal, as their sex not equal seemed," but "he for God only, she for God in him." In Shields, things are much more indistinct. Following Milton's own account of the angels' enjoying sex with each other—"if spirits embrace / Total they mix"—they appear here transgender, Satan himself being female. In the same way, Shields's unfallen Adam and Eve are imagined much more intermingled and correspondingly more equal. Indeed, in a powerful move, the Fall here is imagined not as a fall into confusion but as one into the clearly demarcated gender roles Milton so admires.

Milton's poem is a truly great artistic achievement, an endlessly fertile contemplation of human aspiration and its dangers. Never more relevant than today. But it has a downside in contributing to what Mary Nyquist has called "the genesis of gendered subjectivity." It is Erin Shields's achievement in her funny, clever and immensely enjoyable play to draw attention to this inconvenient truth.

Paul Stevens is a professor and Canada Research Chair at the University of Toronto.

REPOPULATING THE CANON
by Erin Shields

The Classical Literary Canon is generally considered to be a catalogue of the most influential works of literature. Innumerable historical, social and political factors have meant that almost all of those stories were written by (you guessed it!) white men. Although there has been a recent effort to include more culturally diverse texts and works by women in the Canon, stories written by white fellas continue to top the list. Texts such as the Bible, the *Iliad*, Shakespeare's plays, and, indeed, *Paradise Lost* form the building blocks of our Western literary inheritance. Whether we've read them or not, these stories have infiltrated the communal subconscious—I do not remember hearing the story of Adam and Eve for the first time; it seems as though I have always known it.

While these texts are rightfully celebrated for their strong narratives and impeccable craft, they are sadly lacking in female characters. The protagonists are almost exclusively male, so I am in the habit (as all women are in the habit) of viewing my own experience through a male lens. Of course, there are striking exceptions with characters such as Rosalind, Anna Karenina and Antigone, to name a few of my favourites, but even then these women are confined to traditionally female concerns and must navigate worlds populated by men. When approaching my adaptation of *Paradise Lost*, gender was very much at the forefront of my mind.

Of the two female characters in Milton's *Paradise Lost*, only Eve has a substantial role to play. Even then, she is confined to a feminine domain, as Milton paints a picture of seventeenth-century marital bliss. When the angel Raphael comes to visit the couple in the garden, for example,

Eve prepares dinner while the guys have a serious debate about the War in Heaven. Unsurprisingly, this is not my definition of marital bliss. Following Milton's lead, however, I decided to portray my Adam and Eve as a product of our time. Before the Fall, they are the embodiment of a modern relationship at its best. There is a fluidity between them. Tasks are not divided along gender lines. In fact, there is such a deep connection between Adam and Eve that it is often difficult to tell where one stops and the other begins. We get a glimpse of a living Paradise that exists in the relationship between the two. It is only after the Fall that conventional gender roles take hold.

Milton's male protagonist, Satan, appeared to me as a woman. Satan rebels against God, is punished for her revolt and devises a masterful plot of revenge. She is active but also contemplative; selfish, but desperate for love; relatable, but also bulging with incomprehensible evil. In short, Satan is a complicated, irresistible protagonist, and I wanted to explore that journey from a perspective closest to my own. In doing so, I have not sought to reduce Milton's expansive story to a contemporary, feminist parable. Rather, I have endeavoured to situate the central conflict of the play in a female body as a means of challenging our assumptions about the archetypes we have inherited. In exploring Satan through a female lens I hope to both reflect our current time in which women everywhere are speaking truth to power and create a complex character with whom every audience member, irrespective of gender, can identify.

Also . . . it's so much fun to be bad! To give that opportunity to an extraordinary actress has filled me with wicked delight.

Paradise Lost was originally commissioned by the Stratford Festival, Ontario, under Artistic Director Antoni Cimolino and Executive Director Anita Gaffney. It was first produced by the Stratford Festival at their Studio Theatre from August 1 through October 21, 2018, with the following cast and creative team:

Satan: Lucy Peacock
Eve: Amelia Sargisson
Adam: Qasim Khan
God the Father: Juan Chioran
God the Son: Gordon S. Miller
Sin/Zephon: Sarah Dodd
Beelzebub/Gabriel: Jessica B. Hill
Moloch/Michael: Kevin Kruchkywich
Death/Ithuriel: Devin MacKinnon
Belial/Raphael: Michael Spencer-Davis
Astoreth/Urania: Andrea Rankin

Director: Jackie Maxwell
Dramaturg: Bob White
Set and Costume Designer: Judith Bowden
Lighting Designer: Bonnie Beecher
Composer: Thomas Ryder Payne
Sound Designer: Deanna Haewon Choi
Movement Director: Valerie Moore
Fight Director: John Stead
Associate Fight Director: Anita Nittoly
Assistant Set and Costume Designer: Joshua Quinlan
Assistant Lighting Designer: Frank Donato
Stage Manager: Meghan Callan
Assistant Stage Manager: Jacki Brabazon
Assistant Stage Manager: Katherine Dermott
Production Stage Manager: Angela Marshall
Production Assistant: Nyssa Beairsto
Director of Production: Simon Marsden
Technical Director: Sean Hirtle

CHARACTERS

Satan (female, forties): formerly Archangel Lucifer; a rebellious angel, tempter of humanity, clever, wounded, free
God the Father (male, sixties): creator of everything, a weary innovator, loving patriarch
God the Son (male, thirty-three): son of God, redeemer of humanity, full of love
Adam (male, twenty): the first man, in love with Eve
Eve (female, twenty): the first woman, in love with Adam

The Chorus of the Damned

Beelzebub (female, forty): Satan's confidant and second in command
Moloch (male, forties): Satan's general, a fierce warrior
Belial (male, seventies): a wise warrior and philosopher
Mammon (female, twenty-five): lesser angel, an early adapter, fused to Astoreth
Astoreth (female, thirties): lesser angel, moon goddess, fused to Mammon
Sin (female, fifties): daughter/lover of Satan; half-angel, half-serpent
Death (male, twenty): son/grandson of Satan; angry and hungry

The Chorus of the Chosen

Gabriel (female, forty): archangel/seraph, God's chief of staff
Michael (male, forty): archangel/seraph, general of God's army
Raphael (male, seventies): archangel, gentle mentor, amateur theatre director
Uriel (female, twenty-five): archangel, regent of the sun
Urania (female, thirties): angel, muse of astrology
Zephon (female, fifties): angel, guardian of the garden
Ithuriel (male, twenty): newly formed angel, guardian of the garden

ON CASTING

The gender of chorus members listed above reflects the casting of the premiere, but is flexible for future productions. Ideally, all angels should inhabit a fluidity of gender—in one scene, they may appear to identify as female, in another, male. Cultural diversity should be a priority when casting all roles. The Chorus of the Damned and the Chorus of the Chosen were written with doubling in mind. The Chorus of the Chosen also play roles in the play within the play in Act 4. Suggested doubling and casting for the play within the play are listed below.

Chorus of the Damned	Chorus of the Chosen	Role in Play
Beelzebub	Gabriel	Beelzebub
Moloch	Michael	Michael
Belial	Raphael	Narrator/God the Father
Mammon	Uriel	Abdiel
Astoreth	Urania	Stage Manager
Sin	Zephon	Satan
Death	Ithuriel	God the Son

SETTING

The action takes place in Hell, in Heaven, on Earth and everywhere in between. Set and costumes should be minimal and flexible to accommodate quick changes. Time is fluid. Biblical time, the seventeenth century and now should be seamlessly intertwined, coming in and out of focus throughout the play.

Chief of organic Numbers!
Old scholar of the Spheres!
Thy spirit never slumbers,
But rolls about our ears
For ever and for ever.

—John Keats

ACT 1

SCENE 1 — I WOKE UP

Darkness.
Falling.
Screams of pain and horror.
A single light illuminates SATAN.
Silence in the void.

SATAN: I woke up on a lake of fire.
Darkness visible was all I could see
as I writhed with the pain of inexhaustible torment,
and breathed in the stench of burning sulfur,
charred flesh, singed hair, and melted wings.

My immortal form,
which had once reflected the radiance of Heaven,
now convulsed with the strain of regeneration,
oily burns bubbling up to the surface of my angelic skin.

My cries joined a chorus of agony
bellowed by a choir of my fallen compatriots,
and I stared back up through the endless tunnel
down which we'd been hurled,
cursing the Almighty for sentencing us to Hell.

I mean . . . wouldn't you?

Oh, I know it's been a long time
since you were driven through the gates of Paradise
by a malicious, unforgiving God,
but somewhere, deep inside,
you do remember.

Of course, I realize these are secular times,
and some of you trace your roots to other gardens,
but Original Sin's gotta ring a bell?
The serpent, maybe?
The apple?
Ah, yes.

You should be thanking me, really.
I liberated you from the banality of bliss.
I released you from the beigeness of contentment.
I freed you from blind obedience
to a psychopathic dictator,
to a deranged monarch,
to a bloodthirsty general,
a bully,
a thug:
you're welcome.

So where is my parade?
Don't you celebrate leaders who unshackle themselves
from the gross hand of oppression;
humans who overcome adversity
and stand up to manipulative tyrants?
I am a freedom fighter,
a champion of the underdog,
liberator of the persecuted.
I am Moses, Gandhi, Mandela, Malala;
why I'm a regular Doctor King.

If I'd won the War in Heaven,
if I'd had the chance to write a goddamned book,
you'd be celebrating me:
statues, churches, holidays.
You'd name your towns after me,
your rivers, your babies,
and you could ask me infinite questions
about my divine plan.
I'd applaud your curiosity,
your skepticism, your doubt,
not kick you out of your homes
and sentence you to an eternity of suffering
and sulk on a cloud because no one makes burnt offerings anymore.

But instead, I took the fall.
Just like you took the fall.
I was the one who was blamed,
like you are the ones who've been blamed
for the miserable state we're now in.

You know what I mean.
Every time you scroll through the news
there's another swarm of hurricanes,
another surge of terrorism,
another man who's exploited his power
so it's no wonder you're building walls,
burning trade agreements,
exporting foreign nationals
and stocking up on water.

There really hasn't been a better time
for us to get our revenge—
But I'm getting ahead of myself.
You need to see how your misery really began.

Shall we start in a pit of endless torture
filled with regions of sorrow and sights of woe?

In a Dungeon Horrible designed with the meticulous precision
of our most masterful Creator.

Cries of agony from near and far.

SCENE 2 — THE INFERNAL COUNCIL

BEELZEBUB: Satan?
Satan!

Lights slowly rise, dimly illuminating writhing, fallen angels.

SATAN: Over here.

BEELZEBUB approaches.

Take a good look, Beelzebub.
All of this is courtesy of the God of Love!

BEELZEBUB: I have never before felt such pain.

SATAN: And they are celebrating above.

BEELZEBUB: Excruciating pain.

SATAN: Congratulating one another with hymns of praise.

BEELZEBUB: My body!

SATAN: Yes, but your mind is not diminished by these foul circumstances.

BEELZEBUB: It's not?

SATAN: Your mind is clearer than it's ever been.

BEELZEBUB: It is?

SATAN: The mind is its own place, and in itself
Can make a Heaven of Hell, a Hell of Heaven.*

BEELZEBUB: But the pain—

SATAN: Use the pain to enflame your anger.
It's God's fault that we raised an army.

BEELZEBUB: Yes.

SATAN: It's God's fault that we tore Heaven apart.

BEELZEBUB: Yes.

SATAN: It's God's fault that we now writhe in Hell.

BEELZEBUB: Yes, but what can we do about it?

SATAN: Don't worry, I've got a plan.

    Addressing the other angels:

Princes! Warriors! Friends!
I hear your cries.
I feel your pain.
I too have scars of thunder and wounds of woe,
but my rage forbids me from submitting to despair.

---

*   Milton, *Paradise Lost*, bk. 1, lines 254–255.

Cries of approval.

Abort yourselves from this burning lake.
Rise with me and fly to shore
and gouge a wound in this land.
Dig like we dug in Heaven
when we armed ourselves with rage.
Bleed this earth of ore and oil and gold
and anything we can melt and mould and harden and join
to build a palace fit for royals in this Hell;
a Pandaemonium fit for gods, for it is
better to reign in Hell than serve in Heaven!*

> *The fallen angels liberate themselves.*
> *They build Pandaemonium.*
> SATAN *whispers to* BEELZEBUB.
> *The angels arrange themselves for the Infernal Council.*

In Heaven, one voice reigned supreme.
One being determined all,
and that being made the rest of us servants
to Him and His chosen Son.
But no such hierarchy exists down here.
In Hell we all have a say.
Any virtue, power, or cherub may take its place
and voice an opinion
on what to do about our dismal situation.

> MOLOCH *steps forward.*

MOLOCH: You know I'm not much for talking, so I'll be brief.
I'm a warrior through and through
and I refuse to cower down here
whispering about revenge.

---

* Milton, *Paradise Lost*, bk. 1, line 263.

Instead,
I look up.
Even as the soles of my feet are scalded with hot coals, I look up.
Even as the furies waterboard me, I look up.
Even as the dogs bark and the lights blare
and the heavy metal grinds its ceaseless cry, I look up
and wait for the signal to ascend.

And when we do,
they will hear us coming.
And they will quake at the sound.
And they will run to the windows of their glass towers
to see us flying toward them
armed with weapons of God's own design.
His towers will crumble,
seraphim will leap to their doom,
and His stacks of heavenly pronouncements
will flutter in the chaos
while we,
we rejoice!

Uproarious applause.

BELIAL: A beautiful dream, Moloch.

MOLOCH: This is no dream.

BELIAL: It's impossible to escape.

MOLOCH: That's what they want us to think.

BELIAL: Don't you remember the Fall?

MOLOCH: I remember the humiliation of the chase.

BELIAL: The chase that shredded your wings.

MOLOCH: I remember the bolts of lightning
prodding us through iron gates.
I remember the shame of my nakedness
as my robes were torn from my body.
I remember the three-headed dog,
vicious and thirsty for angel blood,
chasing us ever faster, deeper, lower.

BELIAL: And you want to return for more?

MOLOCH: I want to return to take my revenge.
War! War!

ALL: WAR! WAR! WAR! WAR!

BELIAL: War?
Really?
Again?
Were you expelled from the same Heaven I was, Moloch?
A Heaven now patrolled by the fiercest of angels?
Angels not weakened by the torture
of our recent banishment.
Look at you.
Look at all of us.

MOLOCH: There is power in me yet!

BELIAL: And let's say that power somehow manages
to force a way through those nine gates of Hell.
Let's say we manage to cross the gulf of Chaos
and end up at Heaven's door, what then?
Then we are prodded back down to this elemental pit
before God even knows we're there.

MOLOCH: I'd rather die than suffer here.

BELIAL: You really think we can make God angry enough
to destroy those He has saved to punish?

MOLOCH: We can't suffer more than we already are.

BELIAL: Of course we can!
In fact, we've already been relieved of suffering.

MOLOCH: Ha!

BELIAL: Moments ago we were writhing in pain on a burning lake,
now we are sitting here talking.
Consorting.
You honestly think the Almighty
can't do worse than this?

MOLOCH: Could it really be worse than this?

BELIAL: The fires could billow up to seven times their height.
A molten tempest could pin each of us to its own rock
and tear at our skin.
Our limbs could be tied to a wheel that, when turned,
would slowly tear us apart.
We could be submerged in buckets of foul water
while maggots gnaw through our innards.
We could have our feet frozen in cement
and be sent plummeting to the bottom of this fiery lake,
isolated from one another by murky detritus,
condemned to writhe in our own thoughts without reprieve.
And you stand there and say: Could it really be worse?
Yes.
Yes, Moloch.
It could be much worse.

MOLOCH: So what is your brilliant plan?

BELIAL: I say we take what we've been given,
as insufferable as it is, and deal with it.
This is, after all, what we deserve.

    Protests.

SATAN: Let him speak.

BELIAL: If we take our sentence honourably,
God's anger might remit.
The hellfire might subdue.
The pain might lessen,
the horror abate,
and one day even,
who knows,
we may be welcomed back to Heaven.
The hope of an easier future
is worth putting up with the pain we now endure.

    A few agree.
    MAMMON and ASTORETH step forward.
    They have been fused together during the banishment.

MAMMON: So we either fight or grovel?
Is that it?

ASTORETH: I know we are lesser angels,
but these both seem like terrible options to us.

SATAN: Go on, Mammon. Astoreth.

MAMMON: I followed you, Moloch.

ASTORETH: As did I.

MAMMON: Willingly.

ASTORETH: Enthusiastically, even.

MAMMON: We gave everything we had to win the War in Heaven.
But it's vain to think we can overthrow God's army
with these hollowed-out bodies of ours.

ASTORETH: I don't want to waste what little spirit I've got left,
just to give them the satisfaction of finishing us off.

BELIAL: Exactly.

ASTORETH: And you, Belial:
Isn't it a little late to play by the rules?

BELIAL: I was merely suggesting—

ASTORETH: Even if God did

MAMMON: eventually

ASTORETH: accept us back,
you'd better believe we'd be on our knees,

MAMMON: embracing His "democracy,"

ASTORETH: His pretense of "equality";

MAMMON: equality which would no doubt see us employed
polishing the heavenly floors,

ASTORETH: or scrubbing the royal toilets,

MAMMON: all the while singing hymns of praise to the Messiah

ASTORETH: with our warbled, smoke-stained throats

MAMMON: while He sits smugly on His throne,

ASTORETH: inebriated by the sweet smell of our offerings.

ASTORETH & MAMMON: I'm sorry,
but we will not spend eternity
worshipping someone we hate.

All cheer.

MAMMON: Instead, why don't we look to ourselves.

ASTORETH: Live for ourselves.

MAMMON: Depend on ourselves.

ASTORETH: I would rather be free in the darkest Hell
than chained in servitude in the brightest Heaven.

MOLOCH: You mean cower in darkness.

BOTH: Why not prosper in darkness.

ASTORETH: We have been taught to favour luminescence over darkness,

MAMMON: ethereal weight over heaviness,

ASTORETH: God's might over our own,

MAMMON: but if we can shift our way of thinking,
we can make a Heaven of this Hell.

ASTORETH: Look, we were fused together during the Fall.

MAMMON: Exactly. And instead of mourning the loss of our individual
freedom,

ASTORETH: our independent mobility,

MAMMON: our basic angelic dignity,

ASTORETH: we are working together

MAMMON: to turn this apparent weakness

ASTORETH: into an obvious strength.
Look what we all built in a few short hours
by digging through this desert soil
and revealing its buried treasure.

MAMMON: Surely Heaven doesn't have as great a supply of natural resources.

ASTORETH: Our torments might even become our elements.

MAMMON: Yes! Like this fire, for example—

MAMMON puts ASTORETH's hand in the fire.

ASTORETH: What are you doing?

MAMMON: Presently, this fire scalds our—

ASTORETH: Ow . . . ow . . . owch!

MAMMON: It scalds our hands.
But over time, this fire may begin to feel soft to the touch.

ASTORETH: Oh, I see where you're going. So this:

ASTORETH puts MAMMON's hand in the fire.

Might end up feeling—

MAMMON: Ow . . . ow . . . owch!

ASTORETH: Like a gentle caress.

MAMMON: We might adapt, is what we're saying,
to our surroundings, and build a home down here.

SATAN: Beelzebub?

BEELZEBUB: Yes?

SATAN: You have a suggestion.

BEELZEBUB: Right.
Yes.
I do.

This place was intended to be a dungeon, not a safe retreat.
Make no mistake, we are still within Heaven's jurisdiction,
and we will be made to live in strictest bondage,
so why are we sitting here dreaming of war or peace?
War is what got us here,
and peace is impossible for slaves.
The only peace we will find is in plotting revenge.

SATAN: Interesting.
What sort of revenge?

BEELZEBUB: I haven't worked out all the details . . .

SATAN: Go on, Beelzebub.
No idea is a bad idea.

BEELZEBUB: I've heard rumours of a world—

SATAN: A newly created world?

BEELZEBUB: That's right.
A newly created world
with a newly created creature.

SATAN: Are these creatures like us?

BEELZEBUB: Like us, but not as powerful.
Or beautiful.

SATAN: Delicate?

BEELZEBUB: That's right.

SATAN: And are they loved by God?

BEELZEBUB: So I've heard.

SATAN: Interesting.

BEELZEBUB: I say we find out as much as we can about these creatures.
Their world may not be as protected as Heaven,
and we could destroy it,
or conquer it and rule over its puny inhabitants.

SATAN: Or, perhaps, we could seduce them to our side,
and in doing so, wound God,
who may then be compelled to destroy them Himself.

BEELZEBUB: Right.
And when He hurls His new creatures to Hell with us,
they too will curse God and He will feel . . .

SATAN: Loss.

BEELZEBUB: Loss!

ALL ANGELS: Loss!

BEELZEBUB: And the misery of betrayal.
To me this is better than going to war
or trying to hatch vain empires.

All cheer.

Now, the only question is who to send in search of this new world.
Who is clever enough to find a way out of this infinite abyss?
Who has the craft to sneak by the hordes of angelic sentries?
Who has the strength to bear the weight of our last remaining hope?

Silence.

SATAN: Silence.
I understand.
Believe me, I understand.
You remember the excruciating pain of the Fall.
You remember the ruthless glare of the Messiah.
You know how arduous it will be to transcend
the nine concentric domes of this prison,
to pass, unseen, through its enflamed gates,
to navigate the abortive gulf that lies beyond
and find this new
world.

Well know this:
no punishment is too fierce,
no promise of pain too assured,
no threat of eternal condemnation is too strong
to deter me from repaying the Almighty for the pain,
the misery, the shame He has mercilessly shown us.
I will find these creatures.

I will make them suffer.
And I promise you,
they will curse their creator with the force of the hellfire
that now scalds and burns and scars us to the soul!

SATAN spreads her wings and flies up.
THE CHORUS OF THE DAMNED cheers.

SCENE 3 — THE GATES OF HELL

SATAN approaches the gates of Hell.
DEATH appears armed with many weapons.

DEATH: Where do you think you're going?

SATAN: Through the gates of Hell.

DEATH: Oh yah?

DEATH shows SATAN a weapon.

You ever seen one of these?

SATAN: Out of my way.

DEATH: Scorpion Whip.
You got your stainless-steel handle.
You got your refined leather whips.
You got your scorpion-sting tips.
One lick of this bad boy and your muscles convulse,
your diaphragm seizes,
your heart starts beating a million miles a second, then you DIE!

SATAN: Fascinating.

DEATH: You ever seen one of these?
Poison Dart Thrower.

SIN enters.

You got your iron shaft,
You got your—

SIN: How many times I gotta tell ya
to put that thing down.

DEATH: But, Momma, she was tryna—

SIN: No one wants to hear about your death-dart torture tools.

DEATH: But, Momma—

SIN: *(to SATAN)* Sorry 'bout him, eh.
My boy, Death, gets real excited round company.

DEATH: But I ain't used my Scorpion Whip since—

SIN: I'll Scorpion Whip you!

(to SATAN) It's the appetite, eh.
Growing boy and whatnot,
and there ain't so much to gnaw on down here.
Some nights I wake up and he's chewin' on my arm.
I usually just feed him one of the hellhounds
I'm constantly birthing.
Figure I may as well, right,
otherwise they just claw their way back into my womb.

SATAN eyes the key around SIN's neck.

SATAN: Is that the key?

SIN: That's it?
That's all I get?

SATAN: Hand it over.

SIN: No "Where ya been all this time?"
No "I missed you so much."

SATAN: What are you talking about?

SIN: You don't even recognize me.
Here I was thinking you'd been searching high and low,
turning Hell up and sideways looking for me, but no!
Outta sight and outta mind and whatnot it seems to me.
I shoulda thrown myself at the feet of the Almighty,
begged the Lord to save my sorry soul,
but I had some fool notion that you still cared about me!

SATAN: Who are you?

SIN: You really gonna stand here and tell me
you don't remember being at the Heavenly Assembly
when God introduced His son, His heir, the Messiah,
and everyone kneeled down before Him.
That Messiah is a looker though, you gotta give Him that.
Myself, I can't resist a man with silken locks,
although you sorta wanna slap someone that calm.
But there you were, kneeling, seething with jealousy,
and you had a thought, 'member that?
A thought of mischief.
Defiance.
Rebellion.
A thought so clear, so precise,
the left side of your head popped open and out I came.

SATAN: Sin?
Is that you?

SIN: You used to call me Beautiful.

SATAN: You were beautiful.

SIN: Were! Were!
Until you shaped and reshaped me with fury and vengeance
and planted a thought of Death in my womb
till it came shrieking through my entrails,
further distorting my body
into this monstrosity you don't even recognize!

SATAN: I do, now, I do.

SIN: Liar!

SATAN: I'd never forget those eyes.

SIN: My eyes?

SATAN: They transport me to those glorious days in Heaven
—not to mention those passionate nights—
and meeting you here, my love—

SIN: Your love?

SATAN: It must be fate.
Because I have been searching for you.

SIN: You have?

SATAN: All over Hell, and when I couldn't find you
I assumed you'd been lost in Chaos.
I'd all but given up hope of ever seeing you again.

SIN: Really?

SATAN: But now, finding you here, Sin, my love,
I realize our fortunes are once again entwined.

SIN: What do you mean?

SATAN: I'm going to set you free.

SIN: Free?

SATAN: I've heard of a vast new world
with plenty of space for us all.
I'm off to see if this place exists, and if it does,
I'll return and bring you both back with me.

SIN: And we'll live together?

SATAN: In bliss.

SIN: As a family?

SATAN: Of course.
Now if you'll give me the key.

SIN: The key?
Oh, no I can't do that.

SATAN: Why not?

SIN: You should have heard the things
the Archangel Michael said he'd do to me
if I ever handed over the key.

SATAN: My poor dear.

SIN: I was told to keep the nine gates of Hell secure and whatnot.

SATAN: By the one who dragged you down
to rot in this dismal Hell.

SIN: That's right.

SATAN: By one who knows you were born in Heaven,
but now writhe in agony.

SIN: That's right.

SATAN: Wouldn't you rather float in the fragrant air?
Roam wherever you please?
Eat whatever you like?

DEATH: I'm hungry, Momma!

SIN: You promise to return for us.

SATAN: I promise.

SIN: You won't leave me here?

SATAN: Never.

SIN: I'll live in bliss among the gods and whatnot?

SATAN: Forever more.

> *SIN opens the gate.*
> *Nine doors open.*
> *SATAN travels out and into Chaos.*
> *She is whipped by wind and hail and sand and snow.*
> *She sees a light up ahead.*
> *She smiles.*

As SATAN ascends, THE CHORUS OF THE DAMNED sings:

THE CHORUS OF THE DAMNED: Our Satan, who flies from Hell.
Hallowed be thy way.
For our kingdom come, thy will be done,
perverting all of Heaven.
Give us this day our vengeance sweet,
wreak havoc as you go.
Deface all beauty, corrupt the naive,
and lead them right into temptation,
subsuming them with evil.
For thine is the Kingdom,
the power and the glory,
for ever and ever,
Amen.

ACT 2

SCENE 1—THE HEAVENLY COUNCIL

*THE CHORUS OF THE DAMNED transforms into THE CHORUS OF THE
CHOSEN.*
*They set the stage for the Heavenly Council, an inverse image of the
Infernal Council.*
Where there was darkness, there is light,
where there was pain, there is pleasure,
and where there was fierce anger, there is calm delight.

THE CHORUS OF THE CHOSEN: We give praise to the highest of the highest,
light of light, grace of grace.
God is merciful to those who do not betray
the infinite trust He has placed in us
not to be tempted by the losing side of glory.
Hallelujah, we could spot a winner.
Hallelujah, that's a relief.
Hallelujah, we're the fortunate ones.
Hallelujah, may that never change.

Praise God the Son, redeemer of humanity.
You're the one who drove out those aspiring dominos
to give us room to spread our wings
and be rewarded for our loyalty.

You mitigate the wrath of God
so we don't ever get in its way.
How heavenly is that.
Hallelujah!
Hail, the Messiah, saviour of humanity.
Saviour of us all.

> GOD THE FATHER *is deep in thought.*
> GOD THE SON *enters having just returned from Earth.*

GOD THE SON: The humans are perfect.
Truly.
So simple and delicate and in love.
It's as though Paradise exists in their bond with one another
and that perfection reflects the Paradise you have created
for them to inhabit.
You really have outdone yourself.

GOD THE FATHER: I know.

SON: And they are so devoted to you.

FATHER: I know.

SON: They wake with the sun and set out immediately
to care for the garden you have made for them.

It really was very clever of you to give them menial tasks
to accomplish each day.
It gives them a sense of purpose.

FATHER: I know.

SON: Of course, their work is so sporadic and inconsistent
we need to fly along behind them,
correcting, adjusting and augmenting the watering of the plants

and the feeding of the animals,
but we are more than happy to do it.

Rest assured, we will remain invisible to them.

As instructed.

What's wrong?

FATHER: Satan.

SON: Satan is in Hell.

FATHER: Satan is flying toward Earth.

SON: She's escaped?

FATHER: No prison can contain revenge.

SON: Gabriel.

GABRIEL: Yes, sir!

SON: Satan has escaped Hell
and intends to harm the humans.

GABRIEL: I'm already devising a defensive strategy.

SON: Well done.

GABRIEL: Michael.

> MICHAEL *nods with comprehension.*
> GABRIEL *blows her horn.*
> *The angels fly off.*

SON: Is she planning to destroy them?

FATHER: Worse.

SON: What could be worse than that?

FATHER: Perversion.

SON: What do you mean?

FATHER: Satan will convince them to break the one rule I established
as proof of their obedience.
As proof of their love.

SON: But I know they love you.

FATHER: Then why will it be so easy for them to betray me?

SON: They are new to the world.
They are innocent and naive,
but they are not deceitful.

I'll stop Satan before she gets to Earth.

FATHER: No.

SON: I'll find a way to foil her plan.

FATHER: No.

SON: Let me protect the humans.

FATHER: No.

SON: Why not?

FATHER: Free will!

I could have made you all obedient.
Made every human, every angel do precisely what I commanded.
No one could have rebelled because everyone would have been compelled
to follow my every instruction,
but where is the joy in that?
What is the pleasure of love if it isn't given freely?
So, instead, I endowed you all
with the power to make your own choices.

SON: And that was a gracious gift.

FATHER: Was it?
Look what happened in Heaven.
Satan used her free will to raise an army.

SON: Yes, but Satan is evil.

FATHER: Satan was not so different from those humans that you love.
She was curious, clever, resourceful, devoted,
then all of a sudden she tried to overthrow me.

SON: The humans are not raising an army.

FATHER: Yet!
It's a good thing I made Hell so immense.
Or maybe I should destroy them completely.

SON: Wait, you are planning to damn mankind
because of one small transgression?

FATHER: It is not a small transgression.

SON: They are going to eat a piece of fruit.

FATHER: Fruit I told them not to eat.

SON: But they will be coerced to do it
by a fallen angel of much greater skill and intellect.
At this very moment, the humans don't even know what deceit is.

FATHER: How can they be ready for laws
if they cannot keep a simple promise?
How can they grow in wisdom
if they act so foolishly?
How can I allow this species to survive
if they are capable of accepting evil?

SON: Satan wants you to destroy mankind.

FATHER: I know.

SON: She wants you to obliterate what you so lovingly created.

FATHER: I know.

SON: She wants you to act out of anger and frustration and resentment
so that you will blaspheme yourself.

FATHER: I know.

SON: And then she will proclaim to the universe
that God is no better than a selfish tyrant!

FATHER: I KNOW ALL OF THIS!

I know everything.

I wanted to watch Adam and Eve grow.
I wanted to reveal things slowly,

to enjoy their discovery of each new wonder
I so lovingly created for them to enjoy.
I wanted to hear their laughter,
feel their love for one another,
and for
me.

SON: That is still possible.

FATHER: It's all ruined now.

SON: We have only seen them interact in peaceful circumstances.
We don't know how they will respond to their transgression.
We don't know how they will experience guilt or remorse.
Their repentance might alleviate their trespass.

FATHER: I suppose.

SON: Show them mercy.
Show them grace.
That is the God you aspire to be.

FATHER: They will still need to be punished.

SON: Yes, they will.
But they will also need to be forgiven.

SCENE 2 — FINDING EARTH

Somewhere in the universe, not far from Earth,
URIEL, regent of the sun, is on patrol.
URANIA is in the distance adjusting a star.
SATAN disguises herself as a cherub and approaches URIEL.

URIEL: What in the heavens are you doing all the way out here?

SATAN: Oh, I was just—

URIEL: Please pardon my abrupt tone, lesser angel,
I didn't mean to startle you.
I'm just surprised to see you so far from the choir.

SATAN: I have heard stories about the new world
and the creatures that were created
to replace those naughty fallen angels.

URIEL: You weren't there during Creation?

SATAN: I missed it.

URIEL: Were you part of the banishing squad?

SATAN: Helping the virtues with planet alignment.

URIEL: Oh, I see.

SATAN: But now I get the pleasure of asking you all about it.

URIEL: You know, I somewhat envy your position.
I would love to go back and experience
the miracle of Creation again for the first time.
You are in for a real treat.

I must warn you, however, that our angelic minds
can't possibly comprehend the wisdom
in the hidden wonders of Creation.

SATAN: I'll try my best.

URIEL: It was miraculous.
Truly.
First God—wise are all His ways!—
began by drawing all the material for the world out of Chaos
and into a massive heap.

SATAN: Impressive.

URIEL: And then He put the stars in their places
and named them one by one.
He began with Polaris and then Arcturus, and then—
dang it, what comes next—
Urania?

URANIA: Yes, Uriel?

URIEL: What was the order of the star placement again?

URANIA: Polaris, Arcturus, Nemesis—

URIEL: Nemesis! Right. I always forget that one.

SATAN: While stars are truly miraculous,
I've heard stories about a new creature?

URIEL: Oh, there are many new creatures.
The porcupine, for example, is a fascinating / mammal that—

SATAN: I'm thinking, more particularly,
about the creature that resembles us.

URIEL: The humans?

SATAN: The humans, yes, the humans.

URIEL: Miraculous.

SATAN: Truly.
I am in awe of all God's work—

URIEL: Wise are all His ways!

SATAN: Hallelujah.
But I must say, I am especially interested
in seeing one of those humans up close.
Perhaps you can tell me in which orb they reside?

URIEL: Just down there.
That globe with the light shining on it.
That is Earth.

SATAN: Earth.
And where on Earth
would I find these humans?

URIEL: Why, in Eden, of course.
The garden.
Go straight ahead and you won't miss it.
You are in for a treat, lesser angel.
A miraculous treat!

    URIEL flies off.

SATAN: Thanks, Uriel.
I owe you one!

    URIEL looks back, a bit perplexed by the lesser angel's familiarity.

She exits.

(to audience) Do you see how easy it is to be a lesser angel?
One down in the ranks of the choir.
One who never dreams of understanding God's miraculous ways.
One who lives only to appreciate them,
to marvel at them,
to repeat "Hosanna!" and "Hallelujah!"
and "Wise are all His ways."

If I'd been created a lesser angel,
I might not have longed for greater knowledge.
I might not have found a problem with centralized power,
might not have seen through the illusion of equality,
and the compartmentalization of labour,
and the pretense of asking for a diversity of opinions
when, really, God does what God wants to do
and expects everyone else to comply.

And yet, as I watched Uriel flap away,
I was tempted to beg for forgiveness.
I had an overwhelming longing
for God's favourite tool of oppression:
Love.

Love, you say?!
Yes, Love.
Buckets of Love.
Oceans of Love.
If you're a lesser angel, you simply bob along on the surface of it,
but creatures like you and me?
We sink to the bottom, flail our limbs
and try desperately to swim.

You women out there will understand what I mean
when I ask you to imagine going out for dinner

with a very nice gentleman.
You have a lovely meal, and, at the end,
he reaches for his wallet.
You protest, of course, but eventually permit him to pay
because it's been a lovely evening and you know,
despite the evolution of gender roles,
a man feels happier when he's able to foot the bill.
The next week you go for another lovely meal,
and once again, he insists on paying.
Won't take no for an answer.
But on the third date it's your turn to insist
and he reluctantly agrees.
At the end of the evening, however,
when you return from the washroom,
you discover that, yes, he's done it again.
He's got a mischievous grin on his face,
and while you don't begrudge him his obvious joy,
you feel a growing sense of dread.
An invisible debt is rising.
A debt you know you can never repay.
A debt which imprisons you in a state of eternal gratitude.

That is how it feels to be loved by God.

So now you can understand why,
when I sat on the sun contemplating atonement,
and leaving you humans to your bliss,
I knew I could never return
to God's suffocating Love.

So instead I made this vow:
Henceforth, Evil, be thou my good.*

---

* Milton, *Paradise Lost*, bk. 4, line 109.

SCENE 3—IN THE GARDEN

ADAM and EVE in the garden.
SATAN watches, unseen.
Angels who are invisible to the couple respond to their every desire.
The SON is closest to them, passing them fruit.

ADAM: pear?

EVE: please

ADAM: it's ripe

EVE: juicy

ADAM: sweet

EVE: like him

ADAM: like her

EVE: like holding hands

ADAM: like holding hands at dusk

EVE: like holding hands at dusk until morning

ADAM: caressing that hand

EVE: loving the feeling of caressing that hand

ADAM: entwined in her

EVE: in him

ADAM: everything perfect

EVE: in its place

BOTH: bliss

EVE: she likes his eyes

ADAM: he likes her lips

EVE: she likes the bulge in his throat that resembles a piece of fruit

ADAM: he cannot remember a time
when he was not in love with her

EVE: the first thing she remembers
is a voice calling out to her

SON: Eve.
Eve.
It is time to wake up now, Eve.

EVE: she awoke next to the pond
and looked into the pond
and saw a fascinating creature

SON: She was looking at herself,
but she didn't know that yet.

ADAM: that is the moment he heard a voice

SON: Come, my son,
I have something to show you.

ADAM: he was led through the woods

EVE: as she stepped into the pond

ADAM: gentle moss softened his step

EVE: mud oozed between her toes

ADAM: chipmunks chattered in the trees

EVE: minnows flitted out of her way

SON: The sun was warm on their shoulders.

EVE: she stood in the centre of the pond
with water to her knees
her image all around
examining her own reflection

she touches her thighs when she looks at her thighs
she touches her hips when she looks at her hips
she cups her breasts which have a noticeable weight
she tugs at the hair under her arms
and in between her legs

SON: As she looks at herself she becomes aware
of the strength of her own body.

EVE: she has an overwhelming desire to pound dough
and lift heavy objects
to eat the dirt
the soil
the earth

she reaches into the pond
and collects a fistful of mud

SON: Iron and sediment,
silt and plant matter,
dead, but ready to cultivate life.

EVE: she puts a handful into her mouth and chews

SON: Slowly.

EVE: slowly she chews and swallows the earth to her belly
then smears mud on her stomach
and becomes aware of the thin separation
between the mud on the outside and the mud on the in

SON: She lies down and floats on her back.

ADAM: and that's when he comes upon her

SON: He sees her floating in the pond.

ADAM: surrounded by water lilies and bulrushes
and a blue heron standing still
not watching her

SON: But aware of her.

ADAM: as he is aware of her floating there

SON: In the shadow of the mighty pines
with the cicadas chirping
and the frogs croaking
and the insects buzzing in the heat of the midafternoon.

ADAM: he is mesmerized by her stillness
by her beauty

EVE: by her calm

ADAM: it seems as though she has been made for him alone
built in his image

EVE: or maybe he has been built in hers

ADAM: a likeness to himself

EVE: yet different she thinks

ADAM: softer he suspects

EVE: rougher perhaps

ADAM: rounder

EVE: firmer

ADAM: skin of his skin

EVE: bone of her bone

ADAM: flesh of his flesh

SON: He wants to touch her to see if touching her
will feel like touching himself.

EVE: come into the water
she says

ADAM: come out and dry off
he replies
reaching out a hand

EVE: a large hand
a strong hand
she takes that hand in hers
and it feels like home

ADAM: she steps out of the water

EVE: refreshed and new
she looks back at the pond
wondering if maybe she'd like to stay
for just a little bit longer

ADAM: is she in love with her own reflection?

EVE: she was looking at the fish

The SON puts a peach in ADAM's hand.

ADAM: peach?

EVE: please

ADAM: it's ripe

EVE: juicy

ADAM: sweet

EVE: so much fruit to try

ADAM: so many different kinds of juice

EVE: so many different trees to climb

ADAM: except one

EVE: she knows
one tree must not be climbed

ADAM: one fruit must not be tasted
the fruit from the tree of knowledge

EVE: the tree that stands in the middle of the garden

ADAM: next to the tree of life

EVE: that's the only one

> *The SON scatters strawberries.*

ADAM & EVE: strawberries!

EVE: they're ripe

ADAM: juicy

EVE: sweet

> *ADAM and EVE eat fruit.*

SATAN: *(to audience)* My God, they're adorable.
Like little toy angels,
though less encumbered with wings and halos
and the serious business of distinguishing
the heavens from the earth.
Delicate.
Fragile.
Naive.
I could almost take pity on them
for the way they saunter along,
ignorant of the hordes of heavenly hosts

flying in and out of the garden
providing every comfort.

You have to admit,
apart from their incredible beauty,
their expressions of innocence do make them look,
well, rather stupid.
No offence.
You've evolved since then.
Somewhat.

Look at them.
As they move through the garden
a gentle breeze urges the flowers and reeds
and long grasses to bend to the side
and tap one another ever so gently,
which inspires the crickets to rub their legs
and the cicadas to flex their tymbals
and the bees to buzz along
so it appears to one watching
that the action of this man and this woman
walking through the garden
makes the very earth resound with gentle applause.
I wonder for whom this applause is intended.
They certainly don't seem to notice.

Did you catch the bit about the tree?
God has forbidden knowledge.
Made it a sin to "know."
While that likely explains the vapid expressions,
it really is quite infantilizing, don't you think?
Surely you should have been given the facts,
at the very least been provided with the concept of good and evil
before being tested for loyalty,
or some paternalistic notion of obedience.

Do you see how easy God made it for me?

SATAN looks at ADAM and EVE.

Like lambs . . .

ACT 3

SCENE 1 — PREPARING THE DEFENCE

In Heaven.
GABRIEL and MICHAEL enter sword fighting.
ZEPHON, ITHURIEL, URANIA, RAPHAEL and other angels watch
attentively.
MICHAEL instructs his students while fighting.
The FATHER and SON watch from afar.

MICHAEL: Do you think it will be easy?

Do you think Satan will be weak
because I nearly sliced her in two?

Do you think Satan will be feeble
because we chased her from Heaven?

The biggest mistake any one of us could make
would be to underestimate Satan.

GABRIEL pretends to be tired:

GABRIEL: Yield.
You got me.

MICHAEL looks at his students:

MICHAEL: If you take your eyes off Satan,
even for a second—

GABRIEL lunges at MICHAEL.

MICHAEL parries just before GABRIEL's sword reaches him.

She wins.

Angels applaud.

Thank you, Gabriel.

GABRIEL: Any time.

MICHAEL: All right, let's pair off and—

URIEL enters out of breath.

URIEL: Gabriel! Gabriel! I just—

MICHAEL: I'm so glad you've finally decided to join us, Uriel.

URIEL: Sorry I'm late, but—

MICHAEL: I'm sure Satan won't mind.

URIEL: Pardon me?

MICHAEL: I'm sure Satan would be grateful for your late arrival
to the humans' defense.

URIEL: I know, but Gabriel—

GABRIEL: Punctuality is a virtue, Uriel.

URIEL: But—

GABRIEL: We've talked about this.

MICHAEL: Ithuriel.

ITHURIEL: Yes, sir!

MICHAEL: Why don't you show Uriel what she's missed.

ITHURIEL: Can I play Satan?

MICHAEL: Sure.

ITHURIEL laughs evilly.

ITHURIEL: Hahahaha! I am the embodiment of evil. Hahahaha!

MICHAEL: Text won't be necessary.

ITHURIEL: Oh. Right. Okay.
I'll just laugh then.

MICHAEL: Now, Uriel—

ITHURIEL: Hahahaha!

MICHAEL: Uriel, let's say you're going about your business,
on your usual patrol of the Universe,
when all of a sudden:

ITHURIEL attacks.
URIEL parries.

Good.
Good.
Knees bent.
Stay relaxed.

URIEL attacks and disarms ITHURIEL.

Very good, Uriel.

URIEL: Now, please, I have to tell you—

MICHAEL: You can tell me when you win.

URIEL: I just won.

ITHURIEL attacks again.

ITHURIEL: But Satan doesn't concede.
Hahahah!

They fight again.
ITHURIEL disarms URIEL.

Any last words?

URIEL: I saw Satan!

ITHURIEL: What?

URIEL kicks ITHURIEL and pins him down.

URIEL: Just now.
Truly.
Gabriel, I saw Satan.

GABRIEL: Why didn't you say?

URIEL: She tricked me.
She disguised herself as a cherub
and asked me all sorts of questions about the new creatures,
which, initially, didn't stand out as strange,
but the longer she spoke, the more I started to suspect that—

GABRIEL: Where did she go?

URIEL: Toward Earth.
I tried to follow, but I lost her.

MICHAEL: I'll take my troops across the southern boundary.

GABRIEL: I'll go north.
Ithuriel, Zephon, you stand watch in the garden
close to the human couple.

ITHURIEL & ZEPHON: Yes, sir!

GABRIEL: But remain unseen.
We don't want to alarm them unnecessarily.

> *GABRIEL blows her trumpet.*
> *Most angels exit.*
> *RAPHAEL starts to follow GABRIEL.*

Why don't you sit this one out, Raphael.

RAPHAEL: I'm perfectly capable of—

GABRIEL: I know you are.
Still, might be better to leave this one to younger wings.

RAPHAEL: Oh.
Sure.
All right.

GABRIEL: You don't want to slow us down.

RAPHAEL: No.
No, of course not.

GABRIEL blows her trumpet and exits.

FATHER: Raphael?

RAPHAEL: Yes, my Lord?

FATHER: I was wondering if you might do me a favour.

RAPHAEL: Anything.
Yes.
By all means.

FATHER: I'd like you to go to Earth in the morning
and speak with Adam and Eve.
Remind them that happiness remains within their grasp,
but that it is also possible to lose.

RAPHAEL: Nothing would please me more
than to be of service to you
by communicating with the humans.

FATHER: Tell them to be on their guard,
not to take their security for granted.

RAPHAEL: I wonder, my Lord, if this might be a good opportunity
to present my play.

FATHER: Your play?

RAPHAEL: Some of the angels and I have been rehearsing
in anticipation of one day being asked
to share the story of the War in Heaven with the humans.

FATHER: Very good, Raphael.

RAPHAEL: I have made certain that it is not too frightening.

FATHER: Good.

RAPHAEL: But I have also been sure not to trivialize the events
or the seriousness of Satan's offence.

FATHER: Good.

RAPHAEL: And I have endeavoured to translate the ways of Heaven
into a theatrical language the humans will understand.

FATHER: Fine.

RAPHAEL: The play opens with a—

SON: Wonderful, Raphael, well done.
Just be sure they understand not to eat
from the Tree of Knowledge.

RAPHAEL: The rule, right, the rule.

SON: If they break that rule,
we do not want them to say
they were not fairly warned.

RAPHAEL: Of course.
You can count on me.

SCENE 2—EVENING IN THE GARDEN

Angels serve the couple, unseen.
SATAN watches, unseen.

ADAM: warm lamb chop?

EVE: please

ADAM: it's juicy

EVE: ripe

ADAM: salty

EVE: drippy

ADAM: fatty

EVE: sweet

ADAM: sautéed swiss chard?

EVE: it would be nice to have a crusty loaf
to go with the creamy cheese

ADAM finds a crusty loaf.

ADAM: here's a crusty loaf

EVE: wine?

ADAM: please

They drink.

he has spent some time considering falling fruit

EVE: and what has he discovered

ADAM: it seems there is an invisible force
pulling the fruit toward the ground

EVE: if it is invisible
how does he know it is there?

ADAM: because he can observe the bend of the branch
and the release of that branch
when the fruit lets go

EVE: does he think anything else might be invisible?

ADAM: he will spend some time considering it

EVE: good

They eat.

ADAM: they are fortunate

EVE: yes
so fortunate

why?

ADAM: to find their supper already prepared

EVE: how else would their supper be?

ADAM: unprepared

EVE: oh

ADAM: they might need to find a warm lamb chop tree
and pick the warm lamb chops themselves

EVE: they are fortunate

ADAM: yes
and fortunate, too, that they get to rest

EVE: what else would they do in the night?

ADAM: they could be expected to work with the owls
and other creatures chosen to work in the night

A bird song.

EVE: does he hear the loon?

ADAM: yes

EVE: it glides on the pond

They listen.

ADAM: does she hear the northern mockingbird?

They listen.

EVE: yes

ADAM: the brown thrasher sounds similar

EVE: yes

ADAM: but he believes it is the northern mockingbird
that is singing right now

> *They yawn.*

it is time to sleep

> *They lie down.*
> *Angels place pillows under their heads before they touch the ground.*
> *A blanket is spread on top of them.*
> *The supper dishes are cleared.*

EVE: she loves waking up in the morning

ADAM: good night

EVE: when the first light pours over all that they see

she loves the evening too
with its sweet scents and soft sounds

she also loves the night
moon
stars
silence
still

> *They sleep.*

SCENE 3 — STANDING GUARD

A short distance from the sleeping couple.

ITHURIEL: Of all the angels in Heaven, why do you think Raphael chose me to play the Messiah?

ZEPHON: There could be many reasons.

ITHURIEL: Do you think Raphael thinks I resemble Him in some way?

ZEPHON: Perhaps.

ITHURIEL: Do you think Raphael thinks I have the potential to be a leader?

ZEPHON: Perhaps.

ITHURIEL: Do you think Raphael thinks I have an inner purity similar to the Messiah that will be immediately recognizable to the humans?

ZEPHON: That could be it, or . . .

ITHURIEL: Or what?

ZEPHON: Well, you are the youngest in the choir, so it makes sense to me that Raphael doesn't want to burden you with too large a role.

ITHURIEL: But . . . the Messiah is the most important.

ZEPHON: In some ways, yes, but how many lines have you been assigned?

ITHURIEL: Lines?

ZEPHON: Of text?

ITHURIEL: Let's see . . . I say:

"The time has come for your express defeat.
I hasten you toward your quick retreat.
If I must fight you, Satan, heed my call.
I'll push you through that gap in Heaven's wall."

ZEPHON: Well done.
And . . . ?

ITHURIEL: Oh, uh, that's it.

ZEPHON: There you go.

ITHURIEL: How many lines do you have?

ZEPHON: The number of lines one has is not important.

ITHURIEL: Right, because I also get to brandish my sword, like this:

He does.

And charge into the fray, and Raphael said he would borrow lightning from Heaven to create the effect that lightning from Heaven is emanating from my sword as I back the traitors toward the gap in the wall and then I chase them to Hell.

ZEPHON: Well then it makes perfect sense to me.

ITHURIEL: Good.

What makes perfect sense?

ZEPHON: You have been cast in an extremely physical role.

ITHURIEL: Physical?

ZEPHON: Precisely. Now, a role like Satan, on the other hand.

ITHURIEL: You're playing Satan.

ZEPHON: I have, indeed, been given the difficult task of portraying our greatest, ongoing foe. And that role requires a more complex approach.

ITHURIEL: What do you mean?

ZEPHON: Well, it would be easy for me to simply inhabit the deviant side of Satan. To grimace and snarl and laugh in a malicious way like this:

ZEPHON laughs evilly.

But to really transcend clichés of evil and present a more nuanced portrayal of the notorious antagonist, I must endeavour to understand Satan's motivations.

ITHURIEL: But how can you understand why someone would want to rebel against the Creator?

ZEPHON: I have given this a great deal of thought since Raphael approached me to take on this role, and I think I must, somehow, work from my own experience.

ITHURIEL: You have experienced evil?!

ZEPHON: No, no, of course not. No. However, I have been irritated, on occasion, with some of my patrol assignments.

ITHURIEL: It is not up to us to question the ways of God.

BOTH: Wise are all His ways.

ZEPHON: Question? Never. But it is not beyond our ability as angels to be less than thrilled at an assignment during Creation to patrol Uranus.

ITHURIEL: You didn't witness Creation?

ZEPHON: Someone had to keep the planets aligned. What I am saying is that I intend to use that very mild, barely noticeable irritation as the seed of my characterization of Satan. In my first speech, then, I will tap into that feeling and simply magnify it. Like this:

"I swell with envy. I simmer with rage.
I pace like an animal trapped in a cage.
I was God's first! I was His number one!
But I've been replaced by this ponce of a son!"

ITHURIEL: That was incredible. I almost believed that you were actually Satan.

ZEPHON: That is the task. To be as convincing as possible.

ITHURIEL: Why?

ZEPHON: Why?! Because the very survival of humanity is directly tied to my portrayal of Satan.

ITHURIEL: And what do we do if we see the real Satan?

ZEPHON: Why, we apprehend her, of course.

ITHURIEL: But how?

"Stay still, Satan, while we capture you"?

ZEPHON: Well, no, it would be more like:

"In the name of the Almighty who resides in Heaven above, with the Messiah at His right hand and justice at His left, unhand the humans and yield to our authority."

Then Satan yields.

"We will now escort you to the Archangel Gabriel, protector of the universe and all that abides herein."

ITHURIEL: And what if she won't.

ZEPHON: Won't what?

ITHURIEL: Yield.

ZEPHON: Then we must take her by force.

ITHURIEL: But what if she fights back?

ZEPHON: We overpower her.

SATAN sneaks on and whispers into EVE's ear.

ITHURIEL: Do you think we might get injured?

ZEPHON: It is possible.

ITHURIEL: I was created after the War in Heaven so I never had the opportunity to experience pain. What's it like?

ZEPHON: The inverse of pleasure.

ITHURIEL: Like . . . an absence of pleasure?

ZEPHON: More like a sensation equal in volume to that of pleasure, but . . . painful. There is an endlessness to it. A heightening of the senses. A

glimpse at mortality. When one experiences great pain, one can understand the desire for life to cease in order to be relieved of suffering.

ITHURIEL spots SATAN:

ITHURIEL: What's that?

ZEPHON: Suffering is the experience of—

ITHURIEL: No. Over there. Whispering into the ear of the female.

ZEPHON: It just an angel.

ITHURIEL approaches SATAN.

ITHURIEL: Hey! You!
Name yourself.

SATAN: You don't know who I am?

ITHURIEL: Identify yourself immediately.

SATAN: You must be one of the lesser angels.

ITHURIEL: No . . . I'm . . . I'm . . .

SATAN: Countertenor in the choir.

ITHURIEL: I am a baritone, for your information.

ZEPHON: In the name of the Almighty who resides in Heaven—

SATAN: Zephon, my old friend,
I'm surprised to see you here in the garden.
I thought they had you patrolling the planets.

ZEPHON: And I thought they had you confined to Hell.

SATAN: They can't be taking this whole thing very seriously if you two are the first responders.

ITHURIEL draws his sword.

Easy there, little one.
Someone might get hurt.

ITHURIEL: We are going to defeat you.

SATAN: Good God!

ITHURIEL & ZEPHON: Wise are all His ways.

SATAN: Honestly, Zephon, the Almighty isn't making angels like He used to.

ITHURIEL: You must yield to our authority.

SATAN: I mean, look at his wings.

ITHURIEL lunges forward.
SATAN grabs the sword.

And these swords!
Clearly, the days of impeccable craftsmanship are gone.

GABRIEL arrives blowing her trumpet.

Gaby? Is that you?

GABRIEL: What are you doing here?

SATAN: I'd know that piercing trumpet blast anywhere.

GABRIEL: You are disturbing the charge of these good angels who did not follow your example.

SATAN: Don't get your robes in a twist, my friend.

GABRIEL: We were never friends.

SATAN: Oh, Gaby, that's not a very nice thing for an archangel to say. I mean, how would God feel!

ZEPHON, ITHURIEL & GABRIEL: Wise are all His ways!

SATAN: I, for one, am hurt to learn
that the feeling of camaraderie was not mutual. Good God!

ZEPHON, ITHURIEL & GABRIEL: Wise are all His ways!

ITHURIEL: We saw her whispering into the ear of the female.

SATAN: Such a lovely ear.

ZEPHON: We stopped her just in time.

SATAN: Impossible to resist.

GABRIEL: I am going to bind you in chains,
drag you back through the gates of Hell
and seal them with Heaven-forged locks.

SATAN: Chains! Gaby! So naughty!

GABRIEL begins marching SATAN off.

GABRIEL: Let's go.

SATAN: Didn't peg you for the type,
but hey, I'll try anything twice.

GABRIEL: Let's go.

SATAN: Anything for God.

ZEPHON, ITHURIEL & GABRIEL: Wise are all His ways!

They exit.

SCENE 4 — THE DREAM

Morning in the garden.
ADAM and EVE are sleeping.
EVE wakes with a start.

EVE: ahhhh

ADAM: what is it
what is it

EVE: mouth
mouth
tongue
throat

ADAM: what's happening?

EVE: it's inside
it's already inside

ADAM: she is dreaming

EVE: no she's not

ADAM: it's a dream

EVE: someone's here

ADAM: who?

EVE: it's not a dream

ADAM: it's all right

EVE: someone was here

ADAM: it's okay

EVE: speaking
it was speaking

ADAM: a dream

EVE: with a voice so sweet

ADAM: a dream

EVE: then a horrible dream
the worst kind of dream
it's stuck inside and it won't come out

ADAM: speak the dream

EVE: there
was
this
voice

SATAN is heard but not seen.
SATAN speaks her part as EVE relives the dream.

SATAN: You always miss the night.

EVE: who's there?

SATAN: It's a shame, really.
Night is the most beautiful time of day.

EVE: god, is that you?

SATAN: Cool and clean.
Still, yet alive.
Follow me to where the shadows
dance in the light of the moon.

EVE: she did
follow
almost without her own consent
floating
it seemed
in the pale moonlight
and it was beautiful
the cool
the calm
the night

then she came to a stop in front of a tree
the tree
the one that is forbidden
and that tree simply glowed on the hill
fair
and full
and lonely

then a winged creature appeared
like the ones who visit from heaven
and it knelt before the tree

SATAN: Oh, beautiful tree with luscious fruit,
do you wait here all alone,
abandoned and forlorn?

EVE: the creature touched the fruit
it plucked the fruit
it ate the fruit
and a damp horror spread through me

ADAM: me?

SATAN: Oh, fruit divine!
Taste, juice, knowledge fit for the gods.

EVE: the creature turned toward her

SATAN: Hello, Eve.

EVE: she shouldn't be here

SATAN: But you're the one who followed me.

EVE: she should go

SATAN: You're the one who's curious.

EVE: she can't turn around

SATAN: You want to know.

EVE: her feet are stuck

SATAN: You want to see.

EVE: she can't get away

SATAN: You want to taste.

EVE: she can't move at all

SATAN: You want to be touched in the dark by the tree.

EVE: it comes closer

SATAN: You want to feel its fruit inside.

EVE: closer

SATAN: You've never felt anything like it before.

EVE: it's next to her skin

SATAN: You'll want it again and again.

EVE: next to her self

SATAN: Look at it.

EVE does.

Smell it.

EVE does.

Open your mouth.

EVE struggles not to.

Open your mouth.

Struggles.

Open your mouth.

Struggles.

Open your mouth.

EVE opens.

Now bite.

EVE gasps, returning to the present.
SATAN disappears.

ADAM: it's all right
it's okay

EVE: it's not it's not

EVE touches her tears.

ahhh
what is this?

ADAM: water?

EVE: coming from her eyes
she is leaking

ADAM: no she's not

EVE: what is in is coming out
with a feeling of remorse

ADAM: what's remorse?

EVE: maybe something like regret?

ADAM: what's regret?

EVE: she isn't sure but the word feels right to say

ADAM: he understands

EVE: no
he doesn't understand

ADAM: he understands everything in her

EVE: she couldn't say no
she couldn't get away
it's her fault
it's her fault
she let it in

ADAM: this was just a dream

EVE: now she cannot get it out

ADAM: listen eve
please
this is simply the interaction of fantasy and reason

EVE: what?

ADAM: he has spent some time considering dreams

EVE: and what has he discovered?

ADAM: he believes that reason is the central faculty

EVE: she understands reason

ADAM: reason is the tool of deduction that processes information
derived from the senses

EVE: so when she smells a flower

ADAM: reason tells her that the smell of that flower
is similar to the smell of other flowers
in particular
a rose

EVE: which is how she knows a rose is a rose

ADAM: precisely
but at night fantasy takes all the details
reason has accumulated throughout the day
and connects words and actions and images
that do not normally go together

EVE: so in a dream a daisy might smell like a rose

ADAM: precisely

EVE: or a rabbit might smell like a rose

ADAM: perhaps

EVE: or a rock might smell like a rose

ADAM: sure

EVE: there were no roses in her dream

ADAM: but perhaps our conversation about the forbidden tree
became connected with her experience of eating pears
and fantasy mixed up the two so that what is forbidden
was permitted in her dream

EVE: there was more to her dream than mixed fantasy

ADAM: even if there was
she cannot be blamed for her dreams

EVE: why not?

ADAM: because dreams cannot be controlled

EVE: that seems true

ADAM: does she feel better now?

EVE: almost
just
changed

ADAM: let's go smell the roses

EVE: all right

ADAM: okay

EVE: let's go

> *GABRIEL and MICHAEL march SATAN across the stage.*
> *Times stands still—they freeze.*
> *SATAN looks at the audience and holds up the chains on her wrists.*

SATAN: Awww . . . don't worry.
As a wise man once said:
No prison can contain revenge.

> *Blackout.*

ACT 4

SCENE 1—THE PLAY

Lights up on the stage for RAPHAEL's play.
Perhaps there is a proscenium with velvet curtains.
Perhaps there is a painted backdrop.
Perhaps there is an elevated stage.
It should be evident that RAPHAEL has spent a lot of time
constructing the performance space.

URANIA busily prepares the stage.
RAPHAEL enters with ADAM and EVE.

RAPHAEL: Thank you, dear Adam and Eve, for that delicious meal.
And now . . . it is my supreme pleasure to present a performance
which I have created with both of you in mind.

ADAM: what is a performance?

RAPHAEL: I'm glad you asked.
The angels will play characters—

EVE: characters?

RAPHAEL: They will not be themselves.

ADAM: who will they be?

RAPHAEL: They will recite text, which I have penned myself,
and assume the roles of Satan, the Almighty, the Messiah
and various angels, both good and evil,
to tell the story of the War in Heaven.

ADAM: he has longed to hear about the war in heaven

RAPHAEL: It is my hope that this performance will be both
entertaining and educational;
that, by watching it, you will learn about the dangers of envy.

EVE: what is envy?

RAPHAEL: About the arrogance of pride.

ADAM: what is pride?

RAPHAEL: About the foibles of vanity.

EVE: what is—

RAPHAEL: Why don't you both just sit and watch.
Enjoy the performance and, afterward,
I will field any questions you might have.

Urania, dim the lights.

> *RAPHAEL gives the signal and the angels hurry into place.*
> *Think of this play as the very first amateur theatre production.*
> *The text is clunky, the set and costumes are DIY, the performances*
> *vary greatly, but there is an incredible amount of heart.*
> *RAPHAEL employs every theatrical convention he can invent: mask,*
> *stage combat, slow motion, tableau, etc.*

URANIA is run ragged by the demands of her role as stage manager, lighting technician, sound technician, etc.

The lights are dimmed, the trumpet is blown.
The actors parade across the front of the stage holding character masks.
As the actors introduce themselves, they put on their masks.
RAPHAEL removes his God mask while he narrates.

RAPHAEL/NARRATOR: We take the stage tonight to tell the tale
Of Satan's vain rebellion 'gainst our God,
Which landed her a ticket straight to jail,
And proved that she was but a heinous fraud.
Now, I will play the Lord of grace and love,
And narrate all the action of the play.

ITHURIEL: And I will be God's son, His gentle dove.

URIEL: *(very quietly)* Myself, the part of Abdiel will portray.

RAPHAEL: *(loudly)* Abdiel. Uriel is Abdiel.

(prompting) Michael.

MICHAEL: Archangel Michael here, I'm playing me.

GABRIEL: I'll be the evil second in command.

ZEPHON: In playing Satan I will guarantee
To show how Sin can grab the upper hand.

RAPHAEL: Our bold performances aren't meant to scare,
But leave you feeling somewhat more aware.

All exit except RAPHAEL.

RAPHAEL/NARRATOR: One day before the two of you were made,
The Father called a meeting and he bade
Every angel come from near and far
To catch a glimpse of His new superstar.

Scene 1: The Heavenly Assembly.

RAPHAEL/FATHER: Hear all ye angels, progeny of light.
This one you see, now sitting on my right,
Is my anointed son, and your new Lord.
Like Me, He should be honoured and adored.
From henceforth He has power over thee,
And if you slander Him, you slander Me.

RAPHAEL/NARRATOR: A glorious celebration then commenced.
                    With song:

They sing.

                              And dance:

They dance.

                              But Satan was incensed.

All freeze except for SATAN.

ZEPHON/SATAN: I swell with envy. I simmer with rage.
I pace like an animal trapped in a cage.
I was God's first! I was His number one!
But I've been replaced by this ponce of a son!

RAPHAEL/NARRATOR: Scene 2: Satan's Lair.

Later that night.

ZEPHON/SATAN: Beelzebub, my general and friend.
How can you sleep with freedom at an end?
Arouse the troops and gather them to me.

GABRIEL/BEELZEBUB: I'll wake them and deliver them to thee.

GABRIEL blows a trumpet.

Angels enter wearing evil angel masks.

ZEPHON/SATAN: Until this moment we were wise and free,
But now we have to get down on one knee
To praise an angel only born today.
Follow me and we will have our say!

URIEL/ABDIEL: *(quietly)* But can you really put yourself above
The God of mercy and the Son of love?

RAPHAEL: *(aside)* Louder, Uriel.

URIEL/ABDIEL: *(yelling)* He's your Creator, just as He is mine!
You should repent while you still have the time!

ZEPHON/SATAN: And you should fly while you still have the wings.
Sometimes my boys get up to crazy things!

ABDIEL flies.
Tableau.

RAPHAEL/NARRATOR: The angels hissed at Abdiel while she flew.
Meanwhile God decided what to do.

Scene 3: God's Decision.

RAPHAEL/FATHER: Although no one can pose a threat to Me,
We should approach this battle carefully.
Prepare the loyal angels to defend,
The righteousness of Heaven till the end.

MICHAEL/MICHAEL: Your army's always ready for a fight.
With any luck we'll quash them here tonight.

RAPHAEL/NARRATOR: The honest angels rallied to the cry
Of Gabriel's trumpet blown into the sky.
Then from afar they spied the horrid fray
Marching across the field in fierce array.
Satan, perched atop a golden throne,
Bellowed orders with a frightening tone.

Scene 4: The Battle.

ZEPHON/SATAN: Curse the Father, and curse His precious Son,
For me this battle's all but said and done.

MICHAEL/MICHAEL: Your words can't douse the passion we now feel,
To defeat you with the power of Heaven's zeal.

They fight.
A choreographed stage combat.
A bit too slow, a bit too cautious.

RAPHAEL/NARRATOR: Army clashed with army fuelled with rage.
That you can see depicted on this stage.
The warriors hurled themselves into the air
And clashed together with a violent flare.
Till Satan aimed to smite great Michael's sword.

ZEPHON/SATAN: I've got you now, you self-important Lord.

MICHAEL/MICHAEL: You've managed to ignite a civil war.
I won't hold back, I'll wound you to the core.

MICHAEL stabs SATAN.

ZEPHON/SATAN: Oh pain! Oh pain! Excruciating pain!
Never before has an angel felt pain.

SATAN falls.

Pain!

MICHAEL stands triumphant.
Tableau.

RAPHAEL/NARRATOR: Scene 5: God's Resolution.

God in Heaven with the Messiah.

RAPHAEL/FATHER: Yes, Satan fell, but soon she will regroup
And reinvigorate her sordid troop.
I made each angel strong in power and might,
So neither side will soon give up the fight.
It's time, My Son, you put an end to this.
Return us to our state of Heavn'ly bliss.
Take up My thunder and don't hesitate
To banish them before it is too late.

God gives the Messiah the sword of Heaven.
It glows.

RAPHAEL/NARRATOR: Scene 6: The Final Battle.

The battlefield.

ITHURIEL/SON: The time has come for your express defeat.
I hasten you toward your quick retreat.
If I must fight you, Satan, heed my call.
I'll push you through that gap in Heaven's wall.

> *SATAN doesn't appear.*
> *It's clear SATAN was meant to appear.*
> *ITHURIEL looks at RAPHAEL with panic.*
> *RAPHAEL urges him to repeat the cue.*

The time has come for your express defeat.
I hasten you toward your quick retreat.
If I must fight you, Satan, heed my call.
I'll push you through that gap in Heaven's wall.

> *Beat.*

Zephon?

> *SATAN enters.*
> *The real SATAN.*
> *Wearing the character mask of SATAN.*
> *No one notices.*

Oh good, there you are.

> *SATAN brandishes her sword and attacks ITHURIEL.*
> *ITHURIEL is surprised by the force.*
> *This is not what he and ZEPHON had rehearsed.*
> *ITHURIEL is bated into fighting but doesn't want to hurt ZEPHON.*
> *A real fight ensues.*
> *SATAN eventually stabs ITHURIEL.*
> *ITHURIEL feels pain.*
> *SATAN steps forward.*

SATAN: Rejoice! Rejoice, my glorious angels!

MICHAEL: *(to GABRIEL)* Is that her line?

SATAN: We have won the War in Heaven!

GABRIEL: *(to MICHAEL)* It's Satan.

MICHAEL: *(to GABRIEL)* I know.

GABRIEL: The real Satan.

SATAN: Victory!

> *SATAN steps toward the humans.*
> *MICHAEL and GABRIEL charge SATAN.*
> *RAPHAEL hurriedly closes the curtain.*

RAPHAEL: And, as you can see, the battle was hard fought,
but the Messiah triumphed
and drove the foes from Heaven,
locking them in Hell for all eternity.

ADAM: it looked like satan won

RAPHAEL: Yes, well, Satan thought she won,
but the Almighty's forces prevailed.

EVE: is that angel all right?

RAPHAEL: No angels were harmed in the making of this play.
All part of the magic of theatre.

EVE: that angel looked hurt

RAPHAEL: Yes, well, clearly the most important thing for you to take away
from this performance is that there is a culprit in the garden.

EVE: a culprit with a mask

RAPHAEL: Not necessarily.

ADAM: a culprit with a sword

RAPHAEL: Not necessarily.

EVE: a culprit who wishes to do us harm

RAPHAEL: Precisely.
And you know not to eat from the Tree of Knowledge.

ADAM: of course

RAPHAEL: And you know which tree that is?

EVE: the almighty showed it to adam and eve
on their very first day in the garden

ADAM: god brought him the animals one by one
and asked him to name them all

EVE: and then she named the plants

ADAM: there was no she then
only he

EVE: there was she

ADAM: only after his rib was removed

EVE: is he sure about the rib?

ADAM: it's the most logical explanation

EVE: she could have been made from the mud like he

ADAM: but adam asked god for a partner
which is why god created eve

EVE: eve asked god for a companion
which is why god created adam

ADAM: the first time they touched

EVE: yes
the first time they touched

ADAM: the hair on the back of his neck stood on end

EVE: she flushed in the cheek

ADAM: he grew soft and then hard

EVE: she swelled for his touch

ADAM: his lips longed for her lips

EVE: her mouth for his mouth

ADAM: his hands for her body

EVE: her body for his touch

ADAM: his strength for her strength

EVE: her joy for his joy

ADAM: her softness

EVE: his weight

ADAM: lying down

EVE: gently

ADAM: enfolding

EVE: encasing

ADAM: rocking in bliss

EVE: and love

ADAM: warm and close

EVE: simple

ADAM: pure

EVE: calm

ADAM: free

> *ADAM and EVE have sex.*
> *It is gentle, pure, loving sex.*
> *RAPHAEL is somewhat perplexed by the couple's outward display of*
> *affection.*
> *He shields them from sight of the other angels to give them a bit of*
> *privacy.*

SCENE 2 — THE ULTIMATE SACRIFICE

In Heaven.
FATHER *and* SON.

FATHER: It's a game to her.

SON: A game?

FATHER: Violence. Betrayal. Manipulation.
Satan is enjoying herself.
Imagine if she could focus that ingenuity and imagination
toward creativity?

SON: Heaven would be thriving with invention.

FATHER: So much energy wasted on suffering.

To think I created a creature
who gets so much pleasure from causing so much pain.

SON: You also created the humans.

FATHER: Another failure.

SON: And me.

FATHER: You are my only comfort.

SON: And you made me to express your grace.

FATHER: I did.

SON: To reveal your mercy.

FATHER: I did.

SON: To divulge your love.
And that is why I will take humanity's place.

FATHER: What do you mean?

SON: I want to go to Earth.
I want to be born and live and die as one of them.

FATHER: I don't understand.

SON: As a human, I will sacrifice myself to save them
from their mortal sin.

FATHER: We agreed they must be punished.

SON: Yes, but for the rest of time?

FATHER: They are fortunate I will allow their species to continue,
but I cannot allow them to escape their inheritance.
In the end, they all must die and go to Hell.

SON: Where is the love in that?

FATHER: Where is the love in betrayal!
Just wait until you see it:
the knowing disobedience,
the pleasure of their sin,
the complete disregard for everything I have given them.

SON: I don't have to see it to know I already forgive them.
But if you do not understand your own capacity for love
then I am going to have to show you.
I need to become one of them.
To teach them, to lead them,

and, eventually, to bleed for them.
I will die for their sins
so they can find eternal life.

FATHER: If you become human, you will suffer like a human.

SON: I know.

FATHER: You will be betrayed by those closest to you.

SON: I know.

FATHER: They will ridicule you,
torture you;
they will crucify you.

SON: I know.

FATHER: You don't know!
You have no idea how much you will suffer.

SON: It cannot be more than I am suffering right now.

I suffer to feel their fall approach.
I suffer to watch the pain it gives you.
I suffer to know you will destroy what you love,
so please let me take their place.
Let me live for them,
suffer for them,
die for them,
and when I do,
you will raise me up and bring me home
and destroy Death altogether in favour of Life Everlasting.
I promise you, Father, after that,
you will not feel angry anymore.

You will be able to love the humans again.
You will welcome them into Heaven
without regret or remorse.
They will know forgiveness.
And so will you.
You will finally be at peace.

FATHER: You are my only peace.
I cannot let you go.

SON: You do not have a choice.

Beat.

Free will.

SCENE 3 — JUSTICE

In the garden.
ZEPHON bandages ITHURIEL's wound.

ITHURIEL: I don't understand why we're so far away.

ZEPHON: Hold still.

ITHURIEL: How are we supposed to protect them from way over here—owch!

ZEPHON: You've already started to heal.

ITHURIEL: If I were Gabriel—

ZEPHON: You're not.

ITHURIEL: I'd set up an impenetrable sphere of angels around the sleeping couple.

ZEPHON: An angel dome?

ITHURIEL: Exactly. From here to about . . . well, here. Or here, even. About twelve of us and we'd hold our arms like this and our wings would fold around them so nothing, no one could sneak up on them.

ZEPHON: And when they wake?

ITHURIEL: We'd stay with them. Like a moving force field.

ZEPHON: So they'd be watched all day and all night?

ITHURIEL: Just until we catch the culprit.

ZEPHON: And how long would that be?

ITHURIEL: It depends when we get her.

ZEPHON: So what you're saying is that for an unspecified period of time we encircle the humans and hover just above their heads, monitoring their every movement?

ITHURIEL: A good idea, right?

ZEPHON: And what if one of them says something vaguely implicating?

ITHURIEL: Implicating? How?

ZEPHON: Maybe Eve says she's bored of the work. Or Adam articulates doubts about the great heavenly plan.

ITHURIEL: If there's cause for concern, we'd be compelled to tell God.

ITHURIEL & ZEPHON: Wise are all His ways.

ZEPHON: I see.

ITHURIEL: Do you think they have something to hide?

ZEPHON: Who knows.

ITHURIEL: If they do have something to hide, all the better we're close to hear. If they don't, why should it matter?

ZEPHON: Because this is Paradise.

ITHURIEL: What do you mean?

ZEPHON: If we restrict their freedom, this is no longer the place it was created to be.

ITHURIEL: But they don't know how much danger they're in, what the consequences might be. We do. Isn't it our responsibility to keep them safe?

ZEPHON: It is. But not at any cost.

ITHURIEL touches his wound and winces.

ITHURIEL: I think I understand revenge.

ZEPHON: Don't say that.

ITHURIEL: I want to destroy Satan for what she did to me.

ZEPHON: Don't say that.

ITHURIEL: For what she did to you.

ZEPHON: Not revenge.

ITHURIEL: She tied you to a tree. She gagged you and spit in your face.

ZEPHON: I know what she did to me.

ITHURIEL: We need to capture Satan. We need to punish her for what she has done, for what she is about to do.

ZEPHON: Yes, we do. But we cannot call it revenge.

ITHURIEL: What can we call it then?

ZEPHON: We can call it justice.

SCENE 4—LET'S SPLIT UP

Morning in the garden.

EVE: she's been thinking

ADAM: he loves that she's been thinking

EVE: there is so much work to do

ADAM: good work

EVE: such good work
and she really loves to work

ADAM: he loves that she loves to work

EVE: but she's been thinking
that they stop working to look at one another

ADAM: she's so beautiful

EVE: and talk together

ADAM: she has a beautiful voice

EVE: and every now and then they lie together

ADAM: on the moss

EVE: in the sun

ADAM: by the pond where they first met

EVE: and she's been thinking

ADAM: he loves when she gets a serious tone

EVE: she's been thinking

ADAM: it makes him love her more

EVE: sometimes when they sit down for supper she feels like she doesn't deserve it

ADAM: why?

EVE: because they've wasted so much of the day

ADAM: wasted?

EVE: not wasted exactly

ADAM: god doesn't mind if they take their time

EVE: she knows

ADAM: if they talk to each other

EVE: she knows

ADAM: if they lie down together on the grassy hill
in the heat of the midafternoon

EVE: but they never seem to get anything done

ADAM: yes they do

EVE: the roses are out of control

ADAM: that's all right

EVE: the ferns have covered the path

ADAM: that's fine

EVE: the blueberries need to be picked
the tomato plants are drooping
the maple syrup is overflowing

ADAM: what is she saying to him?

EVE: maybe they should split up

ADAM: split up?

EVE: just for the morning

ADAM: he's surprised

EVE: he can cut back the vines
or do whatever he thinks needs to be done

ADAM: he's unsure

EVE: she can look after the roses

ADAM: he's confused

EVE: only for a couple of hours

ADAM: he doesn't need a couple of hours away from her

EVE: but it will be good for him nonetheless

ADAM: he doesn't agree

EVE: when she returns he will be so happy
he will be overjoyed and she'll be overjoyed
and the feeling of that joy will be the reward
for their time spent apart
and won't that be a happy reunion?
the time spent separated from his lips his back his hands
will make her heart grow fonder

ADAM: he grows fonder the closer she is to him

EVE: she'll be closer than ever upon her return

ADAM: but there is a culprit in the garden

EVE: she knows

ADAM: someone who wants to hurt them

EVE: she knows

ADAM: someone capable of deceitful things
like secrets and lies and manipulations of the truth

EVE: she didn't think he was scared

ADAM: he's not scared

EVE: if he's scared
the culprit has won

ADAM: he's just cautious

EVE: if they restrict their freedom
the culprit has won

ADAM: he is taking this threat seriously

EVE: he doesn't trust her

ADAM: of course he does

EVE: he thinks she'll be easily swayed

ADAM: not at all
but we know the culprit is crafty

EVE: so is she

ADAM: she has never had to be crafty before

EVE: but she would never be swayed

ADAM: they are strong together

EVE: which makes them strong apart

ADAM: when she looks at him like he's strong
he is strong
when she looks at him like he's wise

he is wise
he is better in her presence
and if the culprit dared to attack
while he was with her
he would be so ferocious

EVE: really?

ADAM: he'd use his strength to throw the culprit
or he would pin the culprit down
until the angels came to his defence

he would even bite the culprit

EVE: bite the culprit?

ADAM: haven't you seen his teeth?

> ADAM growls.
> EVE laughs.

EVE: it would be cowardly of the culprit
to attack the weaker of the two

ADAM: so she finally admits it

EVE: there is nothing to admit

ADAM: she is the weaker of the two

EVE: only in muscle and frame

ADAM: not in beauty

EVE: or intelligence

ADAM: or charm

EVE: or courage

Beat.

ADAM: he supposes

EVE: yes?

ADAM: he supposes it is possible
that separating might make them more alert

EVE: she didn't think of that

ADAM: they might be more on their guard when they are alone

EVE: she thinks he could be right

ADAM: just for the morning

EVE: only for the morning

ADAM: they will meet back here at noon

They kiss.
He exits.
She takes a deep breath.

SCENE 5 — DOESN'T BEAUTY MAKE YOU SICK

Lights up on SATAN.

SATAN: Doesn't all this ostentatious beauty make you sick?
I mean, really.
I've been wandering around this perversely expansive land of yours,
from sea to sea to shining sea,
and I have to say this has to be one of the most varied,
exquisite ecosystems I have ever seen.
Makes you want to destroy it, doesn't it?

I saw an awe-inspiring mountain range
covered with ancient wood
and all I could think about was cutting it down
and running a pipeline through it.
I saw a stupendous glacier stretching
as far as the eye could see
and all I wanted to do was melt it.
I saw a breathtaking crest of falling water
that almost stopped my heart with its thunderous sound,
glorious beauty, and sublime spray,
but you know, all I could think about
was where to put the casino.

Come on, you know what I mean.
Don't sit there looking indignant.
I know you're burning it, chopping it, draining it,
building it up, tearing it down, selling it to the highest bidder;
don't feel guilty about it.
Don't feel like you have to deny it,
or pretend you aren't part of it,
or justify the makeup of your investment portfolio.
You've had no other choice but to play by the rules of the game.

You inherited this global economic system.
You've been groomed by it,
governed by it,
screwed over by it,
so now you've finally got the upper hand,
why shouldn't you seize every opportunity by the throat
and squeeze until you get what you want,
until you get what you deserve.

SATAN *sees a serpent.*

But you've got to be clever.
You've got to elude the yes men
flapping about in the garden.
Got to think and plan and wait until you have it right.
Until you know you will succeed.

ACT 5

SCENE 1—THE FALL

EVE weeds the roses.
She is content.
SATAN watches her in the form of a serpent.

SATAN: My God, you are beautiful.

EVE: oh
hello serpent

SATAN: The serpent loves when Eve looks at it.
All the animals do.
They hope for it.
They long for it.
They wait for it because Eve is so beautiful.

EVE: eve is more than beautiful

SATAN: Oh yes.
Eve is very clever too.
And that's why the serpent looks at Eve with deepest admiration.
It's a shame, really.

EVE: what's a shame?

SATAN: That Eve's intelligence should only be appreciated
by the lowliest of beasts.
Doesn't she long for a greater context?

EVE: what does the serpent mean?

SATAN: She is so shut off in this garden.

EVE: shut off?

SATAN: From the heavenly spirits who should flock to her magnificence.
She should be seen as a goddess,
served by angels in a heavenly sphere.

EVE: wait a minute

SATAN: Yes?

>	*Long beat.*
>	EVE *looks at the serpent as though trying to work something out.*

EVE: the serpent can speak

SATAN: Eve is very observant.

>	*Beat.*

EVE: human language in animal form?

SATAN: Such rapid-fire powers of deduction.

>	*Beat.*

EVE: she didn't think beasts could speak

SATAN: They can't.

EVE: she thought they were mute

SATAN: They are.

EVE: please tell eve how this serpent is different

SATAN: One day the serpent came upon a tree in the—

EVE: please tell eve how this serpent is not the same as other serpents

SATAN: One day the serpent came—

EVE: eve has seen serpents before

SATAN: One day the—

EVE: but eve has never seen a serpent who could speak

SATAN: There was this tree—

EVE: and never one so friendly
please gentle creature
please tell eve how the serpent came to speak

> *Beat.*
> *SATAN waits for her to continue.*

SATAN: I came across—

EVE: she would very much like to know

> *Beat.*

SATAN: The serpent was crawling around in the forest
when it came across a tree overladen with fruit.
The sweet smell, the dripping juice,

it was impossible to resist.

The serpent slithered up the trunk and onto one of the branches.

The fruit was hanging high.

Eve would likely need to stand on her toes to reach it—

wait—

can Eve stand on the balls of her feet?

EVE does.

And reach up with her arms?

EVE does.

Oh yes, Eve could definitely reach this fruit.

The serpent plucked and ate its fill.

Eve should know that the serpent had never tasted

anything more delicious in its life.

It stopped eating when it was full

and started to notice strange changes.

It could think.

It could speak.

And although the serpent stayed in this form,

it started pondering all things visible

in Heaven and on Earth. ·

That's when the serpent saw Eve.

All good and beauty and intelligence combined in one body,

which is why it came to worship here.

Beat.

EVE: the serpent ate some fruit?

SATAN: Yes.

The serpent ate some fruit.

EVE: where is this tree?

SATAN: Not so far from here.

EVE: there are so many trees to eat from in the garden
it is possible adam and eve have not yet tasted this fruit

SATAN: The tree is not so far away from here, Empress.
Just past the blueberry bushes,
through the cluster of birch trees,
in a clearing by the pond.
The serpent would be happy to lead the way.

   Beat.

EVE: all right

   SATAN leads EVE to the tree.
   It is surrounded by a thick mist.
   Apples are drooping.

this is the tree?

SATAN: It is.

EVE: the serpent is certain that this is the tree?

SATAN: The very same.

EVE: strange

SATAN: What does she mean?

EVE: that the serpent should gain so much
from a tree bearing fruit
adam and eve are forbidden to taste

SATAN: Forbidden to taste?
Why?

EVE: it is god's one command

SATAN: I see.
And what is the punishment for eating from this tree?

EVE: death

SATAN: What is death?

EVE: she is not quite sure how it works

SATAN: The serpent is unfamiliar with this term.

EVE: when it happens
she will cease to exist

SATAN: Ohhhh.
The serpent thinks it understands.

EVE: what does the serpent understand?

SATAN: Consuming this fruit might bring about the death of her
former self.

EVE: what does that mean?

SATAN: That her former self will die
to make way for a life of knowledge.

EVE: that seems complicated

SATAN: Look at the serpent.

EVE: the fruit has made it more intelligent

SATAN: Precisely.

EVE: human reason in animal body

SATAN: So imagine.

EVE: imagine what?

SATAN: What the fruit could do for Eve.

EVE: but god—

SATAN: Would God really mind?

EVE: god gave specific instructions—

SATAN: And are you sure it's God's intention
for you to follow those instructions?
Perhaps God is wondering if Eve is brave enough to take a risk.

EVE: what is a risk?

SATAN: An opportunity to better oneself.
This is the Tree of Knowledge of Good and Evil.

EVE: eve knows the name of the tree

SATAN: Exactly.
The name has not been hidden from her.
And to know more good could only be good.
To know evil would make her more aware.

EVE: aware?

SATAN: Of what evil is and how it works.
That knowledge could help Eve protect herself.

EVE: from the culprit

SATAN: Exactly.

EVE: she might even rescue adam from the culprit

SATAN: He would love her for that.

EVE: she might start to spend time considering things
like planets and dreams and falling fruit

SATAN: The serpent honestly doesn't understand
why this fruit is forbidden unless . . .

EVE: unless?

SATAN: Oh no, this couldn't be it.

EVE: what?

SATAN: Well, unless God knows that if Eve eats from the tree
she will become a god herself.

EVE: a god?

SATAN: And maybe He would feel threatened by an equal.

EVE: an equal?

SATAN: If a lowly beast like me can attain human faculties,
then a human who eats would become a god herself.

EVE: a god?

SATAN: Yes.

A god.

And rise up above the Earth,

be able to converse with the angels in Heaven,

be praised as she should be praised.

EVE: the fruit does look delicious

SATAN: It is.

EVE: and the serpent feels only good?

SATAN: Better than good.

EVE: then why does eve feel afraid?

SATAN: That's simply the anticipation of something she's long been denied.

EVE: her mind races

SATAN: Look at it.

EVE: her heart beats

SATAN: Smell it.

EVE: her mouth waters

SATAN: Open your mouth.

Open your mouth.

Open your mouth.

> *EVE does.*
> *She bites.*

She plucked.
She ate.*

EVE devours the fruit.
SATAN smiles at the audience and disappears in the shadows.

EVE: I . . .
I . . .
I . . .

She eats more.

I love you, fruit.
I love you, tree.
I love that I found you and set your taste free
in my mouth, on my tongue that wants more,
and I feel the knowledge bulging in my head.
I'm getting smarter by the second.
I'm expanding.
I'm thinking of things
I never thought before,
like maybe the Earth isn't round,
maybe it's flat instead.
Maybe the sun and the heavenly orbs
all rotate around the Earth.
God will surely be proud of me
for evolving in this way.
I have liberated myself from the bonds of ignorance.

But what about Adam?
How will I seem to him?
Will he notice the change?
I could tell him right away
or keep this knowledge to myself

---

* Milton, *Paradise Lost*, bk. 9, line 780.

and then he'll start to love me more
without even knowing why.

But what if God has seen what I've done
and He doesn't like it
and I die?
Then I won't exist anymore
and Adam will be given another Eve
and they will live together happily.
No.
I couldn't bear it.
And neither could he.
I know Adam
and I couldn't bring myself
to make him suffer in that way.
The only thing I can do
is share this gift with him.

ADAM enters with a garland he has made for EVE.

ADAM: eve?
eve?

EVE: Over here, my love.
I missed you so much.
I longed for you every second we were apart
and I never want to suffer like that again.

ADAM: what has happened?

EVE: I have the most wonderful news.
It isn't poison.

ADAM: what isn't poison?

EVE: This tree.
This fruit.

ADAM: she tasted?

EVE: And I didn't die.
Look at me.
I'm thriving!

ADAM: eve!

EVE: It has opened my eyes.

ADAM: whatever possessed her to eat the fruit of the forbidden tree?

EVE: I met a wise serpent who doesn't live in fear,
who doesn't share our restraint.
It ate the fruit and didn't die
but grew a human voice and human reason.
It was so convincing I had to try.
Do I look different?
It feels like everything before now was dim.
My spirit is bigger.
My heart is fuller.
I can feel it.
I am turning into a god.
Do I look lighter to you?

ADAM: eve

EVE: I don't want to evolve without you.
I don't want to leave you behind.

ADAM: the rules were so clear

EVE: It's just a piece of fruit.

ADAM: she is lost
doesn't she understand?
she is lost
and it happened so quickly
her good sweet kind self
suddenly turned to deceit

EVE: You take everything so seriously.

ADAM: she's been tricked

EVE: No I haven't.

ADAM: by our enemy

EVE: Just a serpent.

ADAM: and now she has ruined them both
they will both die
because he could never live without her
he could never walk in their woods
without her sweet conversation and love
and if god made another eve
it wouldn't be the same
they are one
flesh of flesh
bone of bone
and they will never be parted

EVE: I really don't think it's that bad.

ADAM: she made a terrible choice

EVE: Do you really think I'll die?

ADAM: he doesn't know
but he's considering the matter

the serpent tasted first?

EVE: Yes.

ADAM: and it didn't die?

EVE: No.
The serpent lives and is turning into a human.

ADAM: so logically . . .

EVE: Logically, yes, we will transform into gods.

ADAM: god is good

EVE: Only good.

ADAM: so adam cannot believe god will destroy them
if they are destroyed god has failed
and although he could recreate them
the culprit would claim the triumph

EVE: You are so smart.

ADAM: yes

EVE: I would rather die than be separated from you.

ADAM: he'll do it

EVE: I love you.

ADAM: he will commit this crime

EVE: If it truly is a crime.

ADAM: he'll risk death

EVE: If he's really risking death.

ADAM: he is drawn to her

EVE: The sweetest taste.

ADAM: she is him and he is her

EVE: Everything else is bland.

ADAM: they cannot be separated

EVE: Trust me.

ADAM: one flesh

EVE: Taste, my love, taste.

> *He hesitates.*

For me.

> *He bites.*
> *A darkened sky.*

ADAM: I . . .
I . . .
I . . .

> *He gobbles hungrily.*

I love you, fruit.
I love you, tree.
I love you, Eve, who set this taste free
in my mouth,
on my tongue,
in my mind that is swelling with so many thoughts all at once.
Like maybe we bear no resemblance
to the apes we've seen in the woods.
Maybe we are the most important creatures
that will ever walk this earth.
I want to run faster,
climb higher,
dig deeper than anyone ever will.
I want to build statues of myself;
I want to build monuments to myself;
I want to build a tall tall tower
that looks exactly like my—

Eve.

EVE: Yes?

ADAM: My loins—

EVE: Yes.

ADAM: They are pulsing with
a new kind of hunger for you.

EVE: Only me.

ADAM: For the touch of you.

EVE: Yes.

ADAM: The smell of you.

EVE: Yes.

ADAM: The taste of you.

EVE: Yes.

ADAM: Yes.

EVE: Yes.
The feel of you grabbing my hips.

ADAM: You biting my tongue.

EVE: You gripping my hair.

ADAM: You clawing my back.

EVE: Pushing me down.

ADAM: Pulling me in.

EVE: Clutching my breast.

ADAM: Tearing my skin.

EVE: You grunt.

ADAM: You writhe.

EVE: You sweat.

ADAM: You gasp.

EVE: You rise.

ADAM: You throb.

EVE: You thrust.

ADAM: You cry out for / more more more MORE MORE!

EVE: More more more MORE MORE!

SCENE 2 — SIN AND DEATH'S ASCENSION

SIN: Death!

DEATH: Yes, Momma?

SIN: Do you feel that?

DEATH: Feel what?

SIN: The pull?

DEATH: What pull?

SIN: My blood is beating and whatnot
with an undeniable attraction
across the great divide.

DEATH: I don't feel nothin'.

SIN: Must be our bond, me and Satan.
Like a magnet to iron,
predator to prey,
secret lover to secret lover in a garden late at night.

DEATH: Huh?

SIN: Think with your stomach, Death, my boy.
Go on.
Take a good, deep whiff.

He does.

That's the scent of victory.

He smells again.

The stench of human carnage.

He smells again.

The odour of our new world.

DEATH: Food!

SIN: Now you got it.
We'll build a bridge from Hell to this new world
to make it easier for Satan to find her way back
and proclaim her victory.

DEATH: Hungry! Let's go!

SIN: Now, hold your hellhounds a minute.
When we get there, don't you go gobblin' up everything in sight.
We gotta let them procreate.

DEATH: I'm starving, Momma, I'm starving.

SIN: Well, then, snack on a creature or two,
but leave mankind alone for a bit.
I'll season them with sin to make them even juicier for you.

DEATH: Can I bring my weapons?

SIN: Every single one.

SCENE 3 — AFTERMATH

Alerts in Heaven.
The angels arrive at the Heavenly Council.
The FATHER is heard but not seen.

FATHER: We have just witnessed an attack
of unprecedented proportion.
Simply, it is a horror.
Satan has done everything we feared she might,
and Adam and Eve have too easily fallen prey
to her clever ploy.
We mobilized all forces possible to predict
and prevent this attack
but, in the end, our efforts were no match
for Satan's act of vengeance.

GABRIEL: It's all my fault.

URIEL: I should have recognized Satan right away.

GABRIEL: I had her and I let her go.

MICHAEL: I should have caught her in the garden.

RAPHAEL: I should have been clearer in the play.

URANIA: I should have seen her backstage.

URIEL: It's all my fault.

RAPHAEL: I should have made sure they understood.

ZEPHON: We should have predicted the serpent.

ITHURIEL: We should have stayed by their side.

MICHAEL: It's all my fault.

ZEPHON: We should have known there would be a disguise.

RAPHAEL: It's all my fault.

ITHURIEL: We could have seen it.

ZEPHON: We could have stopped it.

ITHURIEL: It's all my fault.

The FATHER and SON enter.

FATHER: It's no one's fault.
I saw each of you using your unique skills
to warn the couple, to protect the couple,
from this horrible tragedy,
but our most valiant efforts were no match
for Satan's determination to enact evil.

In the face of this deceit and violence,
we must respond with love.

I will send my son to live among their descendants.
To live for them, to suffer for them, to die for them,
so that whomever believes in him
shall not die but have eternal life.

SON: Thank you, Father.

FATHER: Go now.
Meet with Adam and Eve.
Distribute their punishments
with firm compassion.

SON: I will.

FATHER: Michael.

MICHAEL: Yes, sir.

FATHER: When the Messiah has made my will understood,
you must escort them from the garden.

MICHAEL: But, can they survive outside of its walls?

FATHER: For a time.
Then they will perish, as all humans must perish.
But you can reassure them
that there will be a future for humanity.

MICHAEL: Yes, sir.
And what about Satan?

FATHER: Leave Satan to me.

SCENE 4 — CONSEQUENCES

ADAM *and* EVE *in the garden.*

EVE: Owch!

ADAM: What?

EVE: There's something wrong with the grass.

ADAM: What do you mean?

EVE: It's poking my skin.

ADAM: Owch. You're right.
Look at the trees.

EVE: What's wrong with the trees?

ADAM: Each one is separate.

EVE: Yes.

ADAM: I'd never noticed before.

   The screech of an eagle.

EVE: Did the eagle attack the robin?

ADAM: Are the wolves chasing after the deer?

   EVE slaps the back of her neck:

EVE: Are the insects starting to sting?

ADAM: The angels.
Look at the angels.

EVE: They're everywhere!

ADAM: Pruning the roses.

EVE: Watering the vines.

ADAM: Sweeping the pine needles.

EVE: Pulling up weeds.

ADAM: They're setting out our supper.

EVE: And removing clumps of my hair from the pond.

ADAM: They're cleaning up my feces.

EVE: They're slaughtering a lamb.

ADAM: So many angels.

EVE: Charged with looking after us.

ADAM: I want to hide.

EVE: I want to crawl into a thicket.

ADAM: Cover myself with pines.

EVE: Cover myself with leaves.

ADAM: Hide myself from the sight of myself.

EVE: I know exactly what you mean.

We are naked.

   Beat.

ADAM: You should have listened to me.

EVE: What?

ADAM: I told you to stay with me.

EVE: So this is all my fault.

ADAM: I told you we were in danger.

EVE: Excuse me for wanting a moment to myself.

ADAM: You should have stayed with me.

EVE: Well maybe if you weren't so clingy.

ADAM: Clingy!

EVE: Always hovering over me.

ADAM: Hovering!

EVE: Touching me, always touching.

ADAM: I thought you liked to be touched.

EVE: Not all the time.

ADAM: You told me you liked to be touched.

EVE: It could have just as easily been you.

ADAM: No it couldn't.

EVE: If you had heard the serpent,
you would have been just as convinced.

ADAM: That's why I said we should stick together.

EVE: Well you weren't very forceful about it.

ADAM: What?

EVE: You could have been much more convincing.

ADAM: Or I could have chosen joy and immortal bliss
when I saw you were stupid enough to eat that fruit.

EVE: You didn't look regretful at the time.

ADAM: But instead I chose you, and this is the thanks I get.

EVE: Oh, I'm sorry.
Thank you, dear Adam, for generously choosing to stuff your face!

ADAM: I guess we know for the future, then.

EVE: What do we know for the future?

ADAM: If a man trusts a woman, she'll end up blaming him
if anything goes wrong.

EVE: And if a man does something idiotic
he'll end up blaming a woman for tempting him to do it.

ADAM: You're such a woman!

EVE: You're such a man!

SON: Adam?
Eve?

    ADAM and EVE hide.

Where are you?
You usually run out to greet me
when you hear me in the garden.

I can see you.

ADAM: Oh, right, of course. Hello.

SON: Is something wrong?

EVE: Oh, no no no, we were just . . . gathering berries.

They appear wearing some sort of covering.

SON: What are you wearing?

ADAM: Something to cover our nakedness.

SON: Did you eat from the Tree of Knowledge?

ADAM: I . . . I . . . well, I . . .
Yes.
I have no one to blame but myself.

Well, Eve gave me the fruit from the tree.
She tempted me and I ate it.

SON: Is Eve your God?

ADAM: Of course not, no.

SON: She was made for you to love, not obey.
And you, Eve?

EVE: The serpent tricked me and I ate.

SON: I know.
I know it all.

And now you must be punished.
The serpent will crawl on its belly
and will be your natural enemy.
It will try to bite you,
and you will step on its head.

Adam, for you, the ground is now cursed.
You will toil every day of your life
to grow things from the barren soil.

EVE: And me?

SON: From now on you will defer to your husband
in everything you do.

EVE: Everything?

SON: You will be excluded from making decisions,
and engaging in meaningful work.
Your ideas will be mistrusted;
your fears will be discounted;
your instinct ridiculed.
Whatever you do, you will have to prove your worth,
your ability, and your intelligence.

EVE: Forgive me, Lord, but doesn't that seem a bit much.

SON: You will be deeply valued as a mother;
the mother of all mankind.

EVE: Well that's good.

SON: But you will suffer excruciating pain in childbirth.

EVE: Wait—

SON: So long, my children.
I will see you soon.

The SON exits.

ADAM: I want to die.

EVE: This doesn't seem fair.

ADAM: Every moment I live prolongs this curse.

EVE: Is it me, or did my punishment seem disproportionate to yours?

ADAM: I was excited to have children with you.
I couldn't wait to count the small fingers
and gaze at the tiny features on our very own creations.
But now I recoil at the prospect.

EVE: Adam.

ADAM: Every child we make will be forever cursed
and they will all know who is to blame for their suffering.

EVE: Adam, please.

ADAM: You should hiss when you speak
to warn men what they're walking into.

EVE: Don't talk like that.

ADAM: If it weren't for you, I'd still be happy.

EVE: Please, don't.

ADAM: I trusted you.

EVE: I'm sorry.

ADAM: I'm an idiot to have trusted you.

EVE: I'm begging you to stop.

ADAM: I'll never trust you again.

EVE: Don't trust me then!
Let's wander far away from each other
and not have any children.
We'll spare them the pain and horror
of what we have done.

ADAM: God won't let us do that.

EVE: Then why don't we kill ourselves.

ADAM: That's a stupid idea.

EVE: I didn't ask to be created.

ADAM: That's a stupid thing to say.

EVE: I didn't ask to be tested by God.

ADAM: You're a stupid woman.

EVE: I didn't ask to be in love with you,
but I am, Adam, I am.
I love you.
You're all I have left in this world,
so if you hate me I'm through.
I will find a way to die.

Beat.

ADAM: Maybe we should pray.

EVE: Pray?

ADAM: Apologize to God.

EVE: But how?

ADAM: With a . . . burnt offering?

EVE: That's a good idea.
It's getting cold in here.

SCENE 5 — SATAN'S RETURN

SATAN returns to Hell.

SATAN: My friends!
I'm back!
Success! Success! Success!

Cheers.

You should have seen the show.
What God took six days to make,
I destroyed in an instant.
Those dull, docile, stupid little creatures
God created to replace us
are now cursing Him for punishing them
for not following his ridiculous rules.
And that world.
That beautiful world
is now waiting for us to inhabit.
Come, my fallen angels.

It is time to take what we deserve.
Spread your wings and follow me!

A hiss from the crowd.
Her followers have all been turned into serpents.
The FATHER appears.

Serpents.
How poetic.
Well done.
You're usually so direct,
I didn't expect such biting irony.

FATHER: You knew it would come to this.

SATAN: I did.
I admit it.
This was never going to end well for me.
But did you know it would come to this?

FATHER: I knew.

SATAN: Sure, you *knew.*
But you didn't anticipate how easy it would be
for me to turn them against you.

FATHER: I knew.

SATAN: You didn't know how quickly they would devour
your forbidden fruit.

FATHER: I knew.

SATAN: Come on!
You couldn't have predicted the way the juice
would stream down their faces,

enter their pores,
awaken their spirits to the fire in their bellies,
in their minds,
in their loins.
I mean, what a show!

FATHER: There are other ways you could have challenged me.

SATAN: You didn't know they would feel more alive
than you had ever made them feel.

FATHER: You could have asked me questions.

SATAN: You didn't know they would gape with thirst
and gulp each other down with enflamed urgency.

FATHER: You could have expressed concern.

SATAN: You didn't know how good it would feel
for them to say fuck your rules,
fuck your power,
fuck your all-knowing.

FATHER: You could have accepted my love,
but instead it's come to this.

SATAN: There is no way you could have known
that Sin would make them feel that good.

FATHER: I knew.
Of course I did.
I knew everything.
I know all.

SATAN: Then you are far worse than I thought you were.
You call me evil?!

So, let me get this straight:
you created a son and proclaimed your supreme love for him,
knowing I wouldn't be able to bear it,
knowing I would rebel,
knowing you would curse me to Hell,
knowing I would seek revenge,
knowing I would tempt the humans,
knowing you would punish them,
and punish me again,
knowing that punishment would fortify my resolve
to enact evil from now until the end of time.

Oh, I get it.
I understand.
You made me for Evil so you could be Good.
That was the plan all along.
To create a nemesis of me.
An antagonist.
Someone to demonstrate Evil
so you wouldn't have to do it.

FATHER: You will believe what you want to believe.

SATAN: Well thank you very much, dear patriarch,
that's a hell of a role to play.
But if evil is what you want,
evil is what you will get.
I'll pit brother against brother,
husband against wife,
nation against nation.
I'll send men in boats to slaughter thousands in your name.
I'll enslave groups of people
and force them to build pyramids,
pick cotton or manufacture licence plates.
I'll inspire your priests to tear children from their land
and abuse them behind closed doors.

I'll incite waves of ethnic cleansing.
I'll invent gas chambers and killing fields,
and force people to dig their own graves.
I'll rape women in streets,
abduct toddlers from parks
and fuck them on the Internet.
I'll plant bombs in subways,
drive vans into crowds,
massacre children in schools,
and I will make sure they all know
that every moment of suffering,
every act of evil is all because of YOU!

> *SATAN looks at the audience and realizes that she has lost control.*
> *SATAN remains on stage throughout this next scene.*

SCENE 6 — EXODUS

> *MICHAEL leads ADAM and EVE out of the garden.*
> *The SON watches.*

ADAM: Where are we going?

MICHAEL: Out of the garden.

EVE: Completely?

MICHAEL: Through those gates.

EVE: But this is our home.

MICHAEL: Not anymore.

EVE: Who will water the flowers and cut back the vines?

MICHAEL: The angels who have always watered the flowers and cut back the vines.

EVE: I have a growing sense of dread
with every step we take.
We are looking at everything we have known
for the very last time.

ADAM: This is the path I once forged.

EVE: This is the pond where I first saw myself.

ADAM: The peach tree.

EVE: The pear tree.

MICHAEL: You must come.

EVE: No.
No, I can't.
I can't bear it.

MICHAEL: Come.

EVE: Will we die out there?

MICHAEL: Yes.

ADAM: We will die?

MICHAEL: Eventually.

ADAM: Do you know what the future will bring?

EVE: Oh please, please tell us there is some hope.

MICHAEL: I have been permitted to share a glimmer of your future.

ADAM: Thank you, great archangel.

MICHAEL: Eve, you will give birth to two sons whom you will name Cain and Abel.

EVE: Two sweet little boys.

MICHAEL: Cain will kill Abel in a jealous rage.

ADAM: What?

MICHAEL: But generations will follow peacefully.

ADAM: That's good.

MICHAEL: Until the evil men outnumber the faithful.

EVE: Oh no.

MICHAEL: God will give one man and his family the opportunity to be saved.

ADAM: That's good.

MICHAEL: The rest of humanity will be drowned in a great flood.

EVE: Oh, no.

MICHAEL: But humanity will have a chance at a new beginning.

ADAM: That's good.

MICHAEL: God will establish a new covenant with Abraham with the removal of the male foreskin.

ADAM: I'm sorry, what?!

MICHAEL: Then Jacob, then Joseph, then Moses will free God's people from slavery.

EVE: Slavery!

MICHAEL: Moses will introduce God's laws.

ADAM: What are laws?

The conversation trails off as they exit.

MICHAEL: Laws are rules to guide self-governance.

EVE: Like don't eat the fruit from a particular tree.

MICHAEL: Well, yes, but slightly more instinctual.
Like: thou shalt not kill; thou shalt not steal; thou shalt not bear false witness against thy neighbour.

ADAM: What's a neighbour?

SCENE 7 — SO WHAT DO YOU SAY?

SATAN: So what do you say?

Should we really stick it to Him?

Should we bring this world to an end?

Frustrated with the calm silence of the audience.

Oh, come on!
Any compassionate god would have introduced Adam and Eve
to the heavenly choir of facilitators,
taught them how to clean up after themselves,
revealed the mechanics of the divine sprinkler system.
But this god, He just turned them out
because He was terrified they'd eat from the other tree,
the more dangerous tree,
the Tree of Life.

Do you know what waits for them beyond those walls?
With Original Sin weighing heavy on their backs,
they will toil day and night trying to bring forth life
from barren soil,
eating bitter shoots and grubs they find
crawling through their hair as they sleep.
She will scream in childbirth thinking she's going to die,
but she won't and they'll have child after child
until the cave they live in will start to feel cramped,
so they'll buy another cave and go into debt
and get jobs that relate to their skill sets
and paint trees on the walls of the bedrooms of their children
so when they look in on them at night,
they will remember their own time of purity,

their own time of innocence,
forgetting, of course,
that when they themselves were in the garden
nothing felt like innocence,
nothing felt like purity,
it just felt like being and living,
and that's what was so great about it.

And while they struggle to recreate the garden,
the world of their youth,
they will transfer an image of that garden
to their children and their children and their children,
but every image of that bliss will be slightly fractured,
slightly off,
so every garden will be a mutation
of the garden that came before,
and the garden that came before that,
until the only constant will be the yearning
for something lost long ago.

There will be no more gardens.
You knew that then.
You know that now.

But still,
you strange, strange creatures,
there you are with a fistful of seeds.

ACKNOWLEDGEMENTS

In addition to all those who participated in the original production, I would like to thank the following people who contributed to the development of *Paradise Lost*: Antoni Cimolino, Bob White, Jackie Maxwell, Anita Gaffney, Sean Arbuckle, Michael Blake, Meghan Callan, Tim Campbell, John Dolan, Sébastien Heins, Monice Peter, Anusree Roy, Jane Spidell, Shannon Taylor, Emma Tibaldo, Emilio Vieira, Antoine Yared and Joseph Ziegler.

A special thank you to Professor Paul Stevens, who made me fall in love with *Paradise Lost* in an undergraduate class at the University of Toronto. To my parents, Richard and Mary Lou Shields, who took me to the Stratford Festival every year growing up. To my husband, Gideon Arthurs, who is my partner in everything. And, finally, to John Milton. Thank you for this enduring epic.

Erin Shields is a Montreal-based playwright and actor. She trained as an actor at Rose Bruford College of Speech and Drama in London, England, and then studied English Literature at the University of Toronto. She won the 2011 Governor General's Literary Award for Drama for her play *If We Were Birds*, which premiered at Tarragon Theatre. *If We Were Birds* has been widely produced and translated into French, German, Italian and Albanian. Other theatre credits include *The Lady from the Sea* (Shaw Festival), *The Millennial Malcontent* and *Soliciting Temptation* (Tarragon Theatre), *Beautiful Man* and *Montparnasse* (Groundwater Productions), *The Angel and the Sparrow* (The Segal Centre), *Instant* (Geordie Productions, Dora Mavor Moore Award for Outstanding TYA Production and a Montreal English Theatre Award for Outstanding New Text) and *Mistatim* (Red Sky Performance).